CROCHET

JACKETS, WRAPS & MORE™

EDITED BY
CAROL ALEXANDER

HOUSE of
WHITE
BIRCHES
PUBLISHERS
SINCE 1947

JACKETS, WRAPS & MORE™

EDITOR Carol Alexander
ART DIRECTOR Brad Snow
PUBLISHING SERVICES DIRECTOR Brenda Gallmeyer

ASSOCIATE EDITORS Kristine M. Frye, Lisa M. Fosnaugh
ASSISTANT ART DIRECTOR Nick Pierce
COPY SUPERVISOR Michelle Beck
COPY EDITORS Nicki Lehman, Mary O'Donnell, Susanna Tobias
TECHNICAL EDITOR Agnes Russell

GRAPHIC ARTS SUPERVISOR Ronda Bechinski
GRAPHIC ARTISTS Jessi Butler, Minette Collins Smith
PRODUCTION ASSISTANTS Marj Morgan, Judy Neuenschwander

PHOTOGRAPHY Tammy Christian, Don Clark, Matthew Owen, Jackie Schaffel
PHOTO STYLISTS Tammy Smith, Tammy Steiner

PUBLISHING DIRECTOR David McKee
BOOK MARKETING DIRECTOR Dwight Seward

Printed in China
First Printing 2007

Library of Congress Control Number: 2007921288
Hardcover ISBN: 978-1-59217-153-8
Softcover ISBN: 978-1-59217-190-3

Every effort has been made to ensure the accuracy and completeness of the instructions in this book. However, we cannot be responsible for human error or for the results when using materials other than those specified in the instructions, or for variations in individual work.

1 2 3 4 5 6 7 8 9

DRGbooks.com

A Note From the Editor

Today's fashionable woman
wants it all when it comes
to style and versatility in
her wardrobe.

From classic, traditional pieces to chic, contemporary designs, the variety of fashions and accessories in *Jackets, Wraps & More* will create a look that's just right for any occasion to go from the boardwalk or bistro to the board-room or ballet in perfect style.

Whether your taste caters to bold, colorful expression or sleek, sophisti-cated flair, our impressive array of jackets, wraps, tops, hats, purses, scarves and more will take you from sporty and playful to dazzling and elegant.

This enticing collection includes styles for women of all ages and features a tantalizing mix of yarns and threads in a delicious blend of colors, textures and weights.

With these sensational wardrobe essentials, more is never too much!

Warm regards,

Carol Alexander

CONTENTS

JACKETS 6

WRAPS 50

& MORE 82

JACKETS

Jackets are the must-have essential for any wardrobe.
Our beautiful array of flattering jackets will take you
from classic to contemporary for daytime or evening
with a variety of designs, weights and colors for
perfect year-round style and comfortable wear.

CUT-AWAY CARDI

DESIGN BY LISA GONZALEZ

INTERMEDIATE

Finished Sizes

Instructions given fit 28–30-inch bust (X-small); changes for 32–34-inch bust (small), 36–38-inch bust (medium), 40–42-inch bust (large), 44–46-inch bust (X-large) and 48-50-inch bust (2X-large) are in [ ].

Finished Garment Measurements

Bust: 27–29 inches (X-small) [30–32 inches (small), 34–36 inches (medium), 38–40 inches (large), 42–44 inches (X-large), 46–48-inches (2X-large)]

Gauge

[Sc, ch 5] 4 times = 4 inches; 9 rows = 4 inches

Pattern Notes

Weave in loose ends as work progresses.

Cardigan should be very close fitting.

Cardigan uses net stitch throughout but varies number of chains per stitch to create subtle shaping effect.

There is no right or wrong side due to the nature of the net stitch.

Special Stitch

Net Stitch (net st): Ch 5, [sc in next ch-5 sp, sk next sc, ch 5] across, ending with sc in turning ch, turn.

Materials

- Classic Elite Premiere light (light worsted) weight yarn (1¾ oz/108 yds/50g per hank):
    8 [8, 9, 10, 10, 12] hanks #5291 robin's egg
- Size G/6/4mm crochet hook or size needed to obtain gauge
- Yarn needle
- 12 x 15mm decorative shank button

CARDIGAN

Back

Row 1: Loosely ch 63 [71, 79, 87, 95, 103], ch 5, sk first 2 chs of foundation ch, [sc in next ch, sk next 3 chs, ch 5] across, ending with sc in last ch, turn. *(16 [18, 20, 22, 24, 26] sc, 15 [17, 19, 21, 23, 25] ch-5 sps) (St count does not include turning ch here and throughout.)*

Row 2: Work in **net st** (see Special Stitch) across.

Rows 3–6: Rep row 2.

Row 7: Ch 4, [sc in next ch sp, ch 4] across, ending with sc in turning ch, turn.

Rows 8–15: Rep row 7.

Row 16: Ch 3, [sc in next ch sp, ch 3] across, ending with sc in turning ch, turn.

Rows 17–20: Rep row 16.

Rows 21–31: Rep row 7.

Rows 32–44: Rep row 2.

Armhole Shaping

Row 45: Ch 1, sc in first sc, 4 sc in next ch-5 sp, ch 5, [sc in next ch-5 sp, sk next sc, ch 5] across omitting last ch-5 sp and sc in turning ch, turn.

Row 46: Ch 5, [sc in next ch-5 sp, sk next sc, ch 5] across, ending with sc in last ch-5 sp, leaving group of last 5 sc unworked, turn. *(14 [16, 18, 20, 22, 24] sc, 14 [16, 18, 20, 22, 24] ch-5 sps)*

Row 47: Rep row 2.

Row 48: Rep row 45.

Row 49: Rep row 46. *(12 [14, 16, 18, 20, 22] sc, 12 [14, 16, 18, 20, 22] ch-5 sps)*

Row 50: Rep row 2.

Rows 51–58: Rep row 7. At the end of row 58 for sizes X-small, small, medium and large, fasten off.

For Size X-Large Only
Rows 59 & 60: Rep row 7. At the end of Row 60, fasten off.

For Size 2X-Large Only
Rows 59–62: Rep row 7. At the end of Row 62, fasten off.

Front

Make 2.
Row 1: Loosely ch 19 [23, 27, 31, 35, 39], ch 5, sk first 2 chs of foundation ch, [sc in next ch, sk next 3 chs, ch 5] across, ending with sc in last ch, turn. *(5 [6, 7, 8, 9, 10] sc, 4 [5, 6, 7, 8, 9] ch-5 sps)*
Row 2: Ch 5, [sc in next ch-5 sp, sk next sc, ch 5] across, ending with sc in turning ch, ch 5 and sc again in turning ch, turn. *(6 [7, 8, 9, 10, 11] sc, 5 [6, 7, 8, 9, 10] ch-5 sps)*
Row 3: Work in net st across.
Rows 4 & 5: Rep row 3.
Row 6: Rep row 2. *(7 [8, 9, 10, 11, 12] sc, 6 [7, 8, 9, 10, 11] ch-5 sps)*
Row 7: Ch 4, [sc in next ch sp, sk next sc, ch 4] across, ending with sc in turning ch, turn.
Rows 8 & 9: Rep row 7.
Row 10: Rep row 7, working (sc, ch 4, sc) in last ch-4 sp, turn. *(8 [9, 10, 11, 12, 13] sc, 7 [8, 9, 10, 11, 12] ch-4 sps)*
Rows 11–13: Rep row 7.
Row 14: Rep row 10. *(9 [10, 11, 12, 13, 14] sc, 8 [9, 10, 11, 12, 13] ch-4 sps)*
Rows 15–18: Rep row 7.
Row 19: Ch 3, [sc in next ch sp, sk next sc, ch 3] across, ending with sc in turning ch, turn.
Rows 20–23: Rep row 19.
Rows 24–31: Rep row 7.
Rows 32–44: Rep row 3.

Armhole Shaping
Row 45: Ch 1, sc in first sc, 4 sc in next ch-5 sp *(armhole edge)*, ch 5, [sc in next ch sp, sk next sc, ch 5] across, ending with sc in last ch-5 sp, leaving turning ch unworked, turn.
Row 46: Ch 5, [sc in next ch sp, sk next sc, ch 5] across,

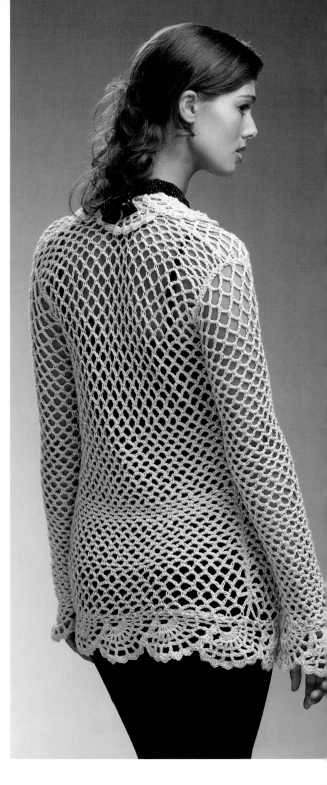

ending with sc in 2nd sc of 4-sc group, turn. *(8 [9, 10, 11, 12, 13] sc, 7 [8, 9, 10, 11, 12] ch-5 sps)*
Row 47: Rep row 3.
Row 48: Rep row 45.
Row 49: Rep row 46, ending with sc in last ch-5 sp and leaving turning ch unworked, turn. *(6 [7, 8, 9, 10, 11] sc, 5 [6, 7, 8, 9, 10] ch-5 sps)*

Row 50: Rep row 3.

Rows 51–58: Rep row 7. At the end of row 58 for sizes X-small, small, medium and large, fasten off.

For Size X-Large Only

Rows 59 & 60: Rep row 7. At the end of row 60, fasten off.

For Size 2X-Large Only

Rows 59–62: Rep row 7. At the end of row 62, fasten off. Holding Back to Front and working through both thicknesses, sc shoulders tog. Matching sts, sc side seams tog.

Sleeve

Make 2.

Row 1: Loosely ch 47 [51, 51, 55, 59, 67], ch 5, sk first 2 chs of foundation ch, [sc in next ch, sk next 3 chs, ch 5] across, ending with sc in last ch, turn. *(12, [13, 13, 14, 15, 17] sc, 11 [12, 12, 13, 14, 16] ch-5 sps)*

Row 2: Work in net st across.

Rows 3–5: Rep row 2.

Row 6: Ch 4, [sc in next ch sp, sk next sc, ch 4] across, ending with sc in turning ch, turn.

Rows 7–30: Rep row 6.

Row 31: Ch 3, [sc in next ch sp, sk next sc, ch 3] across, ending with sc in turning ch, turn.

Rows 32–44: Rep row 31. At the end of row 44, for size X-small only, fasten off.

For Sizes Small, Medium Only

Rows 45–48: Rep row 31. At the end of row 48, fasten off.

For Size Large Only

Rows 45–52: Rep row 31. At the end of row 52, fasten off.

For Size X-Large Only

Rows 45–54: Rep Row 31. At the end of row 54, fasten off.

For Size 2X-Large Only

Rows 45–58: Rep row 31. At the end of row 58, fasten off.

Edging

Note: For each Sleeve, work 3 [3, 3, 4, 4, 5] rep of Edging.

For Body, work 22 [22, 22, 23, 24, 25] rep of Edging. After completing, check to be sure each section of Edging is long enough.

First Edging Repeat

Row 1: Ch 8, sl st to join in first ch, ch 3, 9 dc in ring, turn.

Row 2: Ch 4 *(counts as first dc, ch-1)*, dc in next dc, [ch 1, dc in next dc] 8 times, turn.

Row 3: Ch 5 *(counts as first dc, ch-2)*, dc in next dc, [ch 2, dc in next dc] 8 times, turn.

Row 4: Ch 6 *(counts as first dc, ch-3)*, dc in next dc, [ch 3, dc in next dc] 8 times, turn.

Row 5: Ch 1, [(sc, hdc, dc, hdc, sc) in next ch-3 sp] 9 times, turn.

Additional Edging Repeat

Row 6: Ch 8, sk next sc, sk next hdc, sl st in next dc, turn.

Rows 7–10: Rep rows 2–5 of First Rep of Edging. Continue to rep Additional Edging. Repeat until Edging, as indicated in note, is completed, ending last rep with row 5.

Edging

Row 1: Working along edge that will be attached to Cardigan, ch 5, *sc in top of last dc of row 3, ch 2, sc in 3rd ch of row 2, ch 2, sc in top of last dc of row 1, ch 2, sc in ring, ch 2, sc in last dc of row 4 of previous rep, rep from * along Edging, ending with (sc, ch 2, sc) in beg ch-8 ring of row 1 of First Edging Repeat, fasten off.

Attaching Edging

With RS facing, working through both thicknesses, ch 3, working in ch-3 sps, *insert hook through Edging ch sp and through Sleeve ch sp and complete sc, ch 3, sk next sc on Sleeve and Edging, rep from * until Edging is attached.

Finishing

Sew button to inside edge at junction of joining of Front and Edging about level with beg of armhole. For buttonhole, use natural ch sp on opposite edge. ∎

VERY VICTORIAN

DESIGN BY SUE CHILDRESS

INTERMEDIATE

Finished Size

Instructions given fit most
    women sizes small–large.

Finished Garment
Measurements

Chest: 40 inches

Back neck length: 17 inches

Neck to armhole: 7 inches

Neck to bottom of sleeve:
    7 inches

Gauge

6 dc = 1 inch; 3 dc rows = 1 inch; 4 shell rows = 2 inches

Pattern Notes

Weave in loose ends as work progresses.
Join rounds with a slip stitch unless otherwise stated.

Special Stitches

Shell: (2 dc, ch 2, 2 dc) in indicated st.

V-stitch (V-st): (Dc, ch 1, dc) in indicated st.

Beginning V-stitch (beg V-st): Ch 4 *(counts as first dc, ch-1)*, dc in same st as beg ch-4.

Double shell: (2 dc, ch 2) twice, 2 dc indicated st.

Large shell: (3 dc, ch 2, 3 dc) in indicated st.

Scallop: 9 dc in indicated st.

Materials

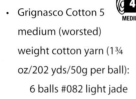

- Grignasco Cotton 5 medium (worsted) weight cotton yarn (1¾ oz/202 yds/50g per ball):
    6 balls #082 light jade
- Size D/3/3.25mm crochet hook or size needed to obtain gauge
- Tapestry needle
- ¾ x 2-inch rhinestone clasp closure
- Stitch marker

JACKET

Body

Row 1: Beg at neckline, ch 140, dc in 3rd ch from hook, dc in each rem ch across, turn. *(138 dc)*

Row 2: Ch 3 *(counts as first dc)*, dc in each of next 2 dc, [2 dc in next dc, dc in each of next 3 dc] 33 times, dc in each of next 2 dc, turn. *(170 dc)*

Row 3: Ch 3, dc in next 4 dc, [2 dc in next dc, dc in each of next 5 dc] 27 times, dc in each of next 3 dc, turn. *(197 dc)*

Row 4: Ch 3, dc in each of next 7 dc, [2 dc in next dc, dc in each of next 6 dc] 26 times, dc in next 7 dc, turn. *(223 dc)*

Row 5: Beg V-st *(see Special Stitches)* in first dc, [ch 1, sk next 2 dc, **shell** *(see Special Stitches)* in next dc, ch 1, sk next 2 dc, **V-st** *(see Special Stitches)* in next dc] across, turn. *(37 shells, 38 V-sts)*

Row 6: Sl st into ch-1 sp of beg V-st, beg V-st in same ch-1 sp, [ch 1, shell in ch-2 sp of next shell, ch 1, V-st in ch-1 sp of next V-st] across, turn.

Rows 7–12: Rep row 6.

Row 13: Sl st into ch-1 sp of beg V-st, beg V-st in same ch-1 sp, [ch 1, shell in ch-2 sp of next shell, ch 1, V-st in ch-1 sp of next V-st] 5 times, ch 1 *(front)*, **double shell** *(see Special Stitches)* in ch-2 sp of next shell, [ch 1, V-st in ch-1 sp of next V-st, ch 1, shell in ch-2 sp of next shell] 6 times, ch 1, V-st in ch-1 sp of next V-st, ch 1 *(sleeve)*, double shell in ch-2 sp of next shell, [ch 1, V-st in ch-1 sp of next V-st, ch 1, shell in ch-2 sp of next shell] 11 times, ch 1, V-st in ch-1 sp of next V-st, ch 1 *(back)*, double shell in ch-2 sp of next shell, [ch 1, V-st in ch-1 sp of next V-st, ch 1, shell in ch-2 sp of next shell] 6 times,

ch 1, V-st in ch-1 sp of next V-st, ch 1 *(sleeve)*, double shell in ch-2 sp of next shell, [ch 1, V-st in ch-1 sp of next V-st, ch 1, shell in ch-2 sp of next shell] 5 times, ch 1, V-st in ch-1 sp of next V-st *(front)*, turn.

Row 14: Sl st into ch-1 sp of beg V-st, beg V-st in same ch-1 sp, [ch 1, shell in ch-2 sp of next shell, ch 1, V-st in ch-1 sp of next V-st] 5 times, *ch 1, shell in first ch-2 sp of next double shell, ch 1, V-st between next 2 dc, ch 1, shell in ch-2 sp of next ch-2 sp of same double shell*, [ch 1, V-st in ch-1 sp of next V-st, ch 1, shell in ch-2 sp of next shell] 6 times, ch 1, V-st in ch-1 sp of next V-st, rep between *, [ch 1, V-st in ch-1 sp of next V-st, ch 1, shell in ch-2 sp of next shell] 11 times, ch 1, V-st in ch-1 sp of next V-st, rep from * to *, [ch 1, V-st in ch-1 sp of next V-st, ch 1, shell in ch-2 sp of next shell] 6 times, ch 1, V-st in ch-1 sp of next V-st, rep from * to *, [ch 1, V-st in ch-1 sp of next V-st, ch 1, shell in ch-2 sp of next shell] 5 times, ch 1, V-st in ch-1 sp of next V-st, turn.

Row 15: Sl st into ch-1 sp of beg V-st, beg V-st in same ch-1 sp, [ch 1, shell in ch-2 sp of next shell, ch 1, V-st in ch-1 sp of next V-st] 6 times, ch 1, **scallop** *(see Special Stitches)* in ch-2 sp of next shell, [ch 1, sc in ch-1 sp of next V-st, ch 1, scallop in ch-2 sp of next shell] 7 times, [ch 1, V-st in ch-2 sp of next shell, ch 1, shell in ch-2 sp of next shell] 13 times, ch 1, V-st in ch-1 sp of next V-st, [ch 1, scallop in ch-2 sp of next shell, ch 1, sc in ch-1 sp of next V-st] 7 times, ch 1, scallop in ch-2 sp of next shell, [ch 1, V-st in ch-1 sp of next V-st, ch 1, shell in ch-2 sp of next shell] 6 times, ch 1, V-st in ch-1 sp of next V-st, turn.

Row 16: Sl st into ch-1 sp of beg V-st, beg V-st in same ch-1 sp, [ch 1, shell in ch-2 sp of next shell, ch 1, V-st in ch-1 sp of next V-st] 6 times, *ch 1, [dc in next dc of 9-dc scallop, ch 1] 9 times, sc in next sc*, rep from * to * across next 7 scallops, [ch 1, V-st in ch-1 sp of next V-st, ch 1, shell in ch-2 sp of next shell] 13 times, ch 1, V-st in ch-1 sp of next V-st, rep from * to * across next 8 scallops, [ch 1, V-st in ch-1 sp of next V-st, ch 1, shell in ch-2 sp of next shell] 6 times, ch 1, V-st in ch-1 sp of next V-st, turn.

Row 17: Sl st into ch-1 sp of beg V-st, beg V-st in same ch-1 sp, [ch 2, **large shell** *(see Special Stitches)* in ch-2 sp of next shell, ch 2, V-st in ch-1 sp of next V-st] 6 times, *ch 2, sk next dc, [5 dc in next ch-1 sp, sc in next ch-1 sp] 4 times, ch 2, sc in next sc*, rep from * to * across next 8 scallops, [ch 2, V-st in next ch-1 sp of next V-st, ch 2, large shell in ch-2 sp of next shell] 13 times, ch 2, V-st in ch-1 sp of next V-st, turn.

Row 18: Sl st into ch-1 sp of beg V-st, beg V-st in same ch-1 sp, [ch 2, large shell in ch-2 sp of next large shell, ch 2, V-st in ch-1 sp of next V-st] 6 times, ch 5 *(under-arm)*, sk next 8 scallops of sleeve, V-st in ch-1 sp of next V-st, [ch 2, large shell in ch-2 sp of next large shell, ch 1, V-st in ch-1 sp of next V-st] 13 times, ch 5 *(underarm)*, sk next 8 scallops of sleeve, V-st in ch-1 sp of next V-st, [ch 2, large shell in ch-2 sp of next large shell, ch 2, V-st in ch-1 sp of next V-st] 6 times, turn.

Row 19 (RS): Place marker on RS, sl st into ch-1 sp of beg V-st, beg V-st in same ch-1 sp, [ch 2, large shell in ch-2 sp of next large shell, ch 2, V-st in ch-1 sp of next V-st] 6 times, *ch 2, sk next 2 chs of ch-5, large shell in 3rd ch of ch-5, ch 2, sk rem 2 chs of ch-5*, [V-st in ch-1 sp of next V-st, ch 2, large shell in ch-2 sp of next large shell, ch 2] 13 times, V-st in ch-1 sp of next V-st, rep from * to *, V-st in ch-1 sp of next V-st, [ch 2, large shell in ch-2 sp of next large shell, ch 2, V-st in ch-1 sp of next V-st] 6 times, turn.

Row 20: Sl st into ch-1 sp of beg V-st, beg V-st in same ch-1 sp, [ch 2, large shell in ch-2 sp of next large shell, ch 2, V-st in ch-1 sp of next V-st] across, turn.

Rows 21–37: Rep row 20.

Row 38: Sl st into ch-1 sp of V-st, ch 1, sc in ch-1 sp of next V-st, [ch 2, 9 dc in ch-2 sp of next large shell, ch 2, sc in ch-1 sp of next V-st] across, turn.

Row 39: Ch 1, sc in first sc, [ch 3, dc in each of next 9 dc, ch 3, sc in next sc] across, turn.

Row 40: Ch 1, sc in first sc, *ch 3, dc in first dc of 9-dc group, [ch 2, dc in next dc] 8 times, ch 3, sc in next sc, rep from * across, turn.

Rnd 41 (RS): Now working in rounds, ch 1, sc in next sc, *[5 dc in next ch-2 sp, sc in next ch-2 sp] 4 times**, sk next 2 ch-3 sps*, rep from * to * across bottom, ending last rep at **, sk last ch-3 sp, sc in next sc, working up right front of Vest in side edge of V-sts, [5 dc in side edge of next row, sc in side edge of next row] across to neckline edge, working across opposite side of foundation ch, sc in first ch, [**sc dec** *(see Stitch Guide)* in next 2

chs, sc in next ch] across neckline, turn, working back across neckline, ch 1, sc in first sc, [sc dec in next 2 sc, sc in next sc] across neckline, turn, working across neckline, ch 1, sc in first sc, [ch 2, sc in next sc] across to end of neckline, working down left front, sc in side edge of first row, [5 dc in side edge of next row, sc in side edge of next row] across to bottom edge, join in beg sc, fasten off.

Finishing
Sew rhinestone clasp to each side of row 1 of Vest. Press Vest. ∎

LOOPY JACKET

DESIGN BY MARTY MILLER

INTERMEDIATE

Finished Sizes

Instructions given fit 32–34-inch bust *(small)*; changes for 36–38-inch bust *(medium)*, 40–42-inch bust *(large)*, 44–46-inch bust *(X-large)* and 48–50-inch bust *(2X-large)* are in [ ].

Finished Garment Measurements

Bust: 37 inches *(small)* [42 inches *(medium)*, 47 inches *(large)*, 52 inches *(X-large)*, 58 inches *(2X-large)*]

Length: 17½ inches *(small)* [18 inches *(medium)*, 18½ *(large)*, 19 inches *(X-large)*, 21 inches *(2X-large)*]

Sleeve length: 18 inches *(small)* [18 inches *(medium)*, 18 inches *(large)*, 18½ inches *(X-large)*, 18½ inches *(2X-large)*]

GAUGE

11 sts = 4 inches; 15 rows = 4 inches

PATTERN NOTES

Weave in loose ends as work progresses.

Join rounds with a slip stitch unless otherwise stated.

Materials

- Red Heart Plush medium (worsted) weight yarn (6 oz/278 yds/170g per skein):
    5 [6, 7, 7, 8] skeins
    #9103 cream
- Size I/9/5.5mm crochet hook or size needed to obtain gauge
- Tapestry needle
- Stitch markers
- ⅞-inch shell button

4 MEDIUM

Loop stitch is worked with wrong side facing, but loops will be on right side when jacket is completed.

SPECIAL STITCHES

Loop stitch (lp st): Insert hook in next st, wrap yarn around index finger twice, insert hook catching the 2 strands of yarn on index finger and draw through st onto hook, drop lps from index finger, yo, draw through all 3 lps on hook.

Foundation chain (foundation ch): Ch 2, insert hook in first ch of ch-2, yo, draw up a lp, yo, draw through first lp on hook *(this is the foundation ch)*, yo, draw through both lps on hook, *insert hook in foundation ch, yo, draw up a lp, yo, draw through first lp on hook, yo, draw through both lps on hook, rep from * until indicated number of foundation chs are completed.

JACKET

Body

Row 1: Starting at bottom edge, work **foundation ch** *(see Special Stitches)* 96 [116, 128, 144, 160] sts, turn. *(96 [116, 128, 144, 160] foundation chs)*

Row 2 (RS): Ch 1, sc in each st across, turn.

Row 3 (WS): Ch 1, sc in first st, **lp st** *(see Special Stitches)* in each st across to last st, sc in last st, turn.

Rows 4–37 [4–39, 4–41, 4–41, 4–43]: [Rep rows 2 and 3 alternately] 17 [18, 19, 19, 20] times.

Right Front

Row 38 [40, 42, 42, 44]: Ch 1, sc in each of next 23 [28, 31, 35, 39] sts, turn.

Row 39 [41, 43, 43, 45]: Ch 1, lp st in each st across to last st, sc in last st *(center front st)*, turn. *(23 [28, 31, 35, 39] sts)*

Row 40 [42, 44, 44, 46]: Ch 1, sc in each st across, turn.

Row 41 [43, 45, 45, 47]: Ch 1, lp st in each st across to last st, sc in last st, turn.

Row 42 [44, 46, 46, 48]: Ch 1, **sc dec** *(see Stitch Guide)* in next 2 sts, sc in each rem st across, turn. *(22 [27, 30, 34, 38] sc)*

Row 43 [45, 47, 47, 49]: Ch 1, lp st in each st across to last st, sc in last st, turn.

Rows 44–63 [46–67, 48–69, 48–69, 50–75]: [Rep rows 42 and 43 {44 and 45, 46 and 47, 46 and 47, 48 and 49} alternately] 10 [12, 12, 12, 13] times. *(12 [16, 19, 23, 23] sts at end of last rep)*

For Sizes Small, Medium, Large & X-large Only

Row 64 [68, 70, 70]: Ch 1, sc in each st across, turn. *(12 [16, 19, 23] sc)*

Row 65 [69, 71, 71]: Ch 1, lp st in each st across to last st, sc in last st, turn.

Row 66 [70, 72, 72]: Ch 1, sc in each st across, fasten off.

For Size 2X-large Only

Row 76: Rep row 46, fasten off. *([23] sc)*

Back

For All Sizes

Row 38 [40, 42, 42, 44]: Sk 2 sts on last row of Body next to Right Front, attach yarn in next st, ch 1, sc in same st as beg ch-1, sc in each of next 45 [55, 61, 69, 77] sts, turn. *(46 [56, 62, 70, 78] sc)*

Row 39 [41, 43, 43, 45]: Ch 1, lp st in each st across, turn.

Row 40 [42, 44, 44, 46]: Ch 1, sc in each st across, turn.

Rows 41–60 [43–64, 45–66, 45–66, 47–70]: [Rep rows 39 and 40 {41 and 42, 43 and 44, 43 and 44, 45 and 46} alternately] 10 [11, 11, 11, 12] times.

Row 61 [65, 67, 67, 71]: Rep row 39 [41, 43, 43, 45].

Right Shoulder

Row 62 [66, 68, 68, 72]: Ch 1, sc in each of next 12 [16, 19, 23, 23] sts, turn. *(12 [16, 19, 23, 23] sc)*

Row 63 [67, 69, 69, 73]: Ch 1, lp st in each st across, turn.

Rows 64 & 65 [68 & 69, 70 & 71, 70 & 71, 74 & 75]: Rep rows 62 and 63 [66 and 67, 68 and 69, 68 and 69, 72 and 73].

Row 66 [70, 72, 72, 76]: Ch 1, sc in each st across, fasten off.

Left Shoulder

Rows 62–66 [66–70, 68–72, 68–72, 72–76]: Sk next 24 [24, 24, 24, 32] sts on row 61 [65, 67, 67, 71], attach yarn in next st, rep Right Shoulder rows 62–66 [66–70, 68–72, 68–72, 72–76].

Left Front

Row 38 [40, 42, 42, 44]: With last row of Body facing, from Back, sk next 2 sts, attach yarn in next st, ch 1, sc in same st as beg ch-1, sc in each of next 22 [27, 30, 34,

38] sc, turn. *(23 [28, 31, 35, 39] sc)*

Row 39 [41, 43, 43, 45]: Ch 1, sc in first st *(front edge)*, lp st in each rem st across, turn. *(23 [28, 31, 35, 39] sts)*

Row 40 [42, 44, 44, 46]: Ch 1, sc in each st across, turn.

Row 41 [43, 45, 45, 47]: Ch 1, sc in first st, lp st in each rem st across, turn.

Row 42 [44, 46, 46, 48]: Ch 1, sc in each st across to last 3 sts, sc dec in next 2 sts, sc in last st, turn. *(22 [27, 30, 34, 38] sc)*

Row 43 [45, 47, 47, 49]: Ch 1, sc in first st, lp st in each rem st across, turn.

Rows 44–63 [46–67, 48–69, 48–69, 50–75]: [Rep rows 42 and 43 {44 and 45, 46 and 47, 46 and 47, 48 and 49} alternately] 10 [11, 11, 11, 13] times.

For Sizes Small, Medium, Large & X-large Only

Row 64 [68, 70, 70]: Ch 1, sc in each st across, turn.

Row 65 [69, 71, 71]: Ch 1, sc in first st, lp st in each rem st across, turn.

Row 66 [70, 72, 72]: Ch 1, sc in each st across, fasten off.

For Size 2X-large Only

Row 76: Rep row 46, fasten off.

Sleeve

Make 2.

Note: Sleeve is started at wrist area, start increase with one st on row 6, placing away from beginning of row. Work the next 3 rows even, increase on row 10, placing increase 1 st away from end of row. Work in this pattern, 3 rows even, 1 row increase, alternating the end of the

row where the increase is until sleeve has 44 [48, 52, 54, 56] sts then work remainder of the rows even.

Row 1: Work 38 [42, 46, 48, 50] foundation chs, turn.

Row 2: Ch 1, sc in each st across, turn. *(38 [42, 46, 48, 50] sc)*

Row 3: Ch 1, lp st in each st across, turn.

Rows 4 & 5: Rep rows 2 and 3.

Row 6: Ch 1, sc in first st, 2 sc in next st, sc in each rem st across, turn. *(39 [43, 47, 49, 51] sc)*

Row 7: Rep row 3.

Rows 8 & 9: Rep rows 2 and 3.

Row 10: Ch 1, sc in each st across to last 2 sts, 2 sc in next st, sc in last st, turn. *(40 [44, 48, 50, 52] sc)*

Rows 11–13: Rep rows 7–9.

Row 14: Rep row 6. *(41 [45, 49, 51, 53] sts)*

Rows 15–17: Rep rows 7–9.

Row 18: Rep row 10. *(42 [46, 50, 52, 54] sts)*

Rows 22–25: Rep rows 11–14. *(43 [47, 51, 53, 55] sts)*

Row 26: Rep row 10. *(44 [48, 52, 54, 56] sts)*

Row 27: Rep row 3.

Rows 28–70 [28–72, 28–72, 28–74, 28–74]: Rep rows 2 and 3. At the end of last rep, fasten off.

Finishing

With RS tog, whipstitch shoulder seams, sl st Sleeve into armhole smoothly, sl st Sleeve seam closed.

Jacket Trim

Rnd 1: Attach yarn at bottom edge, ch 1, sc evenly spaced around Jacket, working 3 sc in each front lower corner and 2 chs in top right corner where the dec for the neck edge starts *(for the button lp)* and **sc dec** *(see Stitch Guide)* in next 3 sts at back of shoulder, join in beg sc, do not turn.

Rnd 2: Ch 1, sc in each sc around, inc at each front corner and sc dec at the dec of shoulders, work 2 sc in the button lp ch-2 sp, join in beg sc, fasten off.
Sew shell button opposite button lp.

Sleeve Trim

Rnd 1: Attach yarn at Sleeve seam, ch 1, sc in each st around, join in beg sc, fasten off.
Rep on opposite Sleeve. ∎

TABARD JACKET

DESIGN BY MARTY MILLER

INTERMEDIATE

Finished Sizes

Instructions given fit 32–34-
inch bust *(small)*; changes
for 36–38-inch bust
(medium), 40–42-inch bust
(large), 44–46-inch bust
(X-large), 48–50-inch bust
(2X-large) and 52–54-inch
bust *(3X-large)* are in [ ].

Finished Garment Measurements

Bust: 40 inches *(small)*
[43 inches *(medium)*,
46 inches *(large)*, 49 inches
(X-large), 51 inches *(2X-large)*, 54 inches *(3X-large)*]

Length: 22½ inches *(small)*
[23½ inches *(medium)*, 4½
(large), 25½ inches *(X-large)*,
25½ inches *(2X-large)*, 26½
inches *(3X-large)*]

Sleeve length: 18½ inches
(small) [18½ inches
(medium), 19½ inches
(large), 19½ inches *(X-large)*,
19½ inches *(2X-large)*, 19½
inches *(3X-large)*]

Gauge

Size H hook: 3 dc = 1 inch; 2 dc rows or rnds = 1 inch

Materials

- TLC Cotton Plus
  medium (worsted)
  weight yarn (3½ oz/178
  yds/100g per ball):
    5 [6, 7, 8, 9, 10] balls
      #3100 cream *(A)*
    2 [2, 3, 3, 4, 4] balls each
      #3303 tan *(B)* and
      #3503 spruce *(C)*
- Sizes H/8/5mm and
  I/9/5.5mm crochet hooks or
  size needed to obtain gauge
- Tapestry needle
- Stitch markers

Pattern Notes

Weave in loose ends as work progresses.

Join rounds with a slip stitch unless otherwise stated.

Size I hook is used only for beginning chain of
Jacket Back.

Start the Jacket with Back, then work oval Fronts and
connect them to the Back leaving space for the armholes. Then work around these 3 pieces to form the
Collar and front and bottom edges.

Place markers at designated stitches and move markers each row or rnd.

JACKET

Back

Row 1: With size I hook and A, ch 63 [66, 69, 72, 75, 78],
with size H hook *(beg sk 3 chs count as first dc)*, dc in 4th
ch from hook *(beg sk 3 chs count as first dc)*, dc in each
rem ch across, turn. *(61 [64, 67, 70, 73, 76] dc)*

Row 2 (RS): Ch 3 *(counts as first dc)*, dc in each dc
across, turn.

Rows 3–18 [3–20, 3–22, 3–24, 3–24, 3–26]: Rep row
2. At the end of last rep, fasten off.

Front
Make 2.

Row 1: With size H hook and A, ch 21 [24, 27, 30, 33,
36], dc in 4th ch from hook *(beg sk 3 chs count as first
dc)*, dc in each rem ch across to last ch, 6 dc in last ch,
place marker in first and last dc of 6-dc group, working
on the opposite side of foundation ch, dc in each ch
across, turn. *(42 [48, 54, 60, 66, 72] dc)*

do not remove markers. *(90 [102, 114, 126, 132, 144] dc)* With WS of Back and first Front facing out, place the straight edge of Front (ends of rows) and side edge of Back with foundation chs tog at top. From bottom upward toward armhole, sew through both thicknesses for 4 [5, 6, 7, 7, 9] rows. Fasten off. Sew shoulder seam from armhole edge through both thicknesses of 9 [12, 15, 18, 21, 24] sts or approximately 3 [4, 5, 6, 7, 8] inches. Sew 2nd Front on opposite side edge of Back in same manner.

Border

Note: Border is worked in rnds around entire Jacket. Collar shaping begins at top edge of Jacket after dc dec in 2nd st of shoulder seam by working around the posts of dc sts at the top edge of Jacket Back.

Rnd 1: With WS of Jacket facing, starting at the bottom, attach C 1 st to the right of bottom left seam on back, ch 3, dc in each st to first marker, [2 dc in next dc, dc in each of next 8 dc] 6 times, dc in each dc to 1 st before shoulder seam, **dc dec** *(see Stitch Guide)* in last st before seam and in first st of seam, dc dec in 2nd st of shoulder seam and in post of next dc, dc in the post of each dc to 1 st before next shoulder seam, dc dec in last post and shoulder seam, dc dec in shoulder seam and next dc, dc in each dc to next marker, [2 dc in next dc, dc in each of next 8 dc] 6 times, dc in each st to end of rnd, join in 3rd ch of beg ch-3, fasten off, turn.

Note: At the end of rnd 1, there is a 6-st inc at rounded end of each Front and a 4-st dec at the collar. Count the number of sts rem and write this number down.

Rnd 2: Attach A, ch 3, dc in each dc to first marker, [2 dc in next dc, dc in each of next 9 dc] 6 times between markers, dc in each dc to first collar dec, dc dec in dec of rnd 1, dc to next dec of rnd 1, dc dec in next dec of rnd 1, dc in each dc to next marker, [2 dc in next dc, dc in each of next 9 dc] 6 times, dc in each st to end of rnd, join in 3rd ch of beg ch-3, turn. *(10-st inc)*

Rnd 3: Ch 3, dc in each dc to first marker, [2 dc in next dc, dc in each of next 10 dc] 6 times, dc in each dc to next marker on 2nd Front, [2 dc in next dc, dc in each

Row 2 (RS): Ch 3, dc in each dc to first marker, 2 dc in each of next 6 dc, dc in each rem dc, turn. *(48 [54, 60, 66, 72, 78] dc)*

Row 3: Ch 3, dc in each dc to first marker, [2 dc in next dc, dc in next dc] 6 times, sc in each rem dc across, turn. *(54 [60, 66, 72, 78, 84] dc)*

Row 4: Ch 3, dc in each dc to first marker, [2 dc in next dc, dc in each of next 2 dc] 6 times, dc in each rem dc across, turn. *(60 [66, 72, 78, 84, 90] dc)*

Row 5: Ch 3, dc in each dc to first marker, [2 dc in next dc, dc in each of next 3 dc] 6 times, dc in each rem dc across, turn. *(66 [72, 78, 84, 90, 96] dc)*

Rows 6–9 [6–10, 6–11, 6–12, 6–12, 6–13]: [Rep row 5] 4 [5, 6, 7, 7, 8] times working inc of 6 dc between markers on each row, turn. At the end of last row, fasten off,

of next 10 dc] 6 times, dc in each rem dc around, join in 3rd ch of beg ch-3, fasten off, turn. *(12-st inc)*

Rnd 4: Attach B, rep rnd 3, inc 6 dc between each marker on each front evenly spaced across, dc in each rem dc, join in 3rd ch of beg ch-3, fasten off, turn. *(12-dc inc)*

Rnds 5 & 6: With C, rep rnd 4.

Rnd 7: Attach A, rep rnd 4.

Rnd 8: Attach B, rep rnd 4.

Rnds 9 & 10: Attach A, rep rnd 4.

Rnd 11: Attach B, rep rnd 4.

Rnd 12: Attach C, rep rnd 4.

Rnd 13: Attach B, ch 1, **reverse sc** *(see Fig. 1)* in each st around, join in first sc, fasten off.

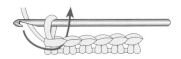
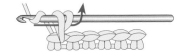

Reverse Single Crochet
Fig. 1

Sleeve

Rnd 1: With WS facing, attach A at underarm, ch 3 *(counts as first dc)*, work 47 [51, 55, 59, 63, 63] dc evenly spaced around armhole opening, join in 3rd ch of beg ch-3, turn. *(48 [52, 56, 60, 64, 64] dc)*

Rnd 2: Ch 3, dc dec in next 2 sts, dc in each rem st around, join in 3rd ch of beg ch-3, turn. *(47 [51, 55, 59, 63, 63] dc)*

Rnds 3–6: Rep rnd 2. *(43 [47, 51, 55, 59, 59] dc at end of last rnd)*

Rnd 7: Ch 3, dc in each dc around, join in 3rd ch of beg ch-3, turn.

Rnd 8: Rep rnd 2. *(42 [46, 50, 54, 58, 58] dc)*

Rnds 9–18: [Rep rnds 7 and 8 alternately] 5 times. *(37 [41, 45, 49, 53, 53] dc)*

Rnds 19–22 [19–22, 19–24, 19–24, 19–24, 19–24]: Rep rnd 7. At the end of last rep, fasten off, turn.

Rnd 23 [23, 25, 25, 25, 25]: Attach C, rep rnd 7, fasten off, turn.

Rnds 24 & 25 [24 & 25, 26 & 27, 26 & 27, 26 & 27, **26 & 27]:** Attach A, rep rnd 7. At the end of last rep, fasten off, turn.

Rnd 26 [26, 28, 28, 28, 28]: Attach B, rep rnd 7, fasten off, turn.

Rnds 27 & 28 [27 & 28, 29 & 30, 29 & 30, 29 & 30, 29 & 30]: Attach C, rep rnd 7. At the end of last rep, fasten off, turn.

Rnd 29 [29, 31, 31, 31, 31]: Attach A, ch 3, dc around, inc 6 [6, 6, 6, 6, 10] dc evenly spaced around, join in 3rd ch of beg ch-3, fasten off, turn. *(43 [47, 51, 55, 59, 63] dc)*

Rnd 30 [30, 32, 32, 32, 32]: Attach B, rep rnd 7, fasten off, turn.

Rnd 31 [31, 33, 33, 33, 33]: Attach A, ch 3, dc around, inc 6 dc evenly spaced around, join in 3rd ch of beg ch-3, turn. *(49 [53, 57, 61, 65, 69] dc)*

Rnd 32 [32, 34, 34, 34, 34]: Rep rnd 7, fasten off, turn.

Rnd 33 [33, 35, 35, 35, 35]: Attach B, rep rnd 31 [31, 33, 33, 33, 33], fasten off, turn. *(55 [59, 63, 67, 71, 75] dc)*

Rnd 34 [34, 36, 36, 36, 36]: Rep rnd 7, do not turn.

Rnd 35 [35, 37, 37, 37, 37]: Ch 1, reverse sc in each st around, join in beg sc, fasten off. Rep on opposite armhole opening. ■

GRANNY SQUARE DRESS & JACKET

DESIGNS BY TAMMY HILDEBRAND

INTERMEDIATE

Finished Sizes

Instructions given fit 32–34-inch bust *(small)*; changes for 36–38-inch bust *(medium)*, 40–42-inch bust *(large)* and 44–46-inch bust *(X-large)* are in [ ].

Finished Garment Measurements

Bust: 36 inches *(small)* [40½ inches *(medium)*, 43 inches *(large)*, 48 inches *(X-large)*]

Gauge

Size E hook: Large Motif = 5 inches square
Size F hook: Large Motif = 6 inches square
Size G hook: Large Motif = 7 inches square

Pattern Notes

Weave in loose ends as work progresses.

Materials

- DMC Senso size 3 crochet cotton (150 yds per ball):

  Dress: 7 [7, 8, 8] balls
  #N1005 terra cotta

  5 [5, 6, 6] balls
  #N1002 ecru

  3 [3, 4, 4] balls each
  #N1012 black and
  #N1004 burnt orange

  Jacket: 4 [5, 6, 6] balls
  #N1005 terra cotta

  2 [2, 3, 3] balls
  #N1002 ecru

  1 [1, 2, 2] balls each
  #N1012 black and
  #N1004 burnt orange

- Sizes E/4/3.5mm, F/5/3.75mm and G/6/4mm crochet hooks or sizes needed to obtain gauge

- Tapestry needle

Join rounds with a slip stitch unless otherwise stated. For shorter length, omit one motif on each strip. For size small, use size E hook; size medium, use size F hook; size large, use size F hook on rounds 1–3 of Large Motifs and size G hook on all other rounds; size X-large, use size G hook.

Alternate colors on Large Motif, round 1 black (ecru), round 2 ecru (burnt orange), round 3 terra cotta (black), round 4 ecru (terra cotta), rounds 5 and 6 burnt orange (ecru). Always alternate placement of Large Motifs, never place 2 of the same color sequence next to one another.

Special Stitches

Chain-3 join (ch-3 join): Ch 1, drop lp, insert hook in center ch of corresponding ch-3 on previous motif, pick up dropped lp and draw through, ch 1.

Chain-5 join (ch-5 join): Ch 2, drop lp, insert hook in center ch of corresponding ch-5 on previous motif, pick up dropped lp and draw through, ch 2.

V-Stitch (V-st): (Dc, ch 1, dc) in indicated st.

DRESS

Large Motif

Rnd 1: Ch 3, join in 3rd ch from hook to form ring, ch 3 *(counts as first dc)*, 15 dc in ring, join in 3rd ch of beg ch-3, fasten off. *(16 dc)*

Rnd 2: Join with sc in any st, 3 dc in next st, [sc in next st, 3 dc in next st] 7 times, join in beg sc, fasten off. *(8 sc, 24 dc)*

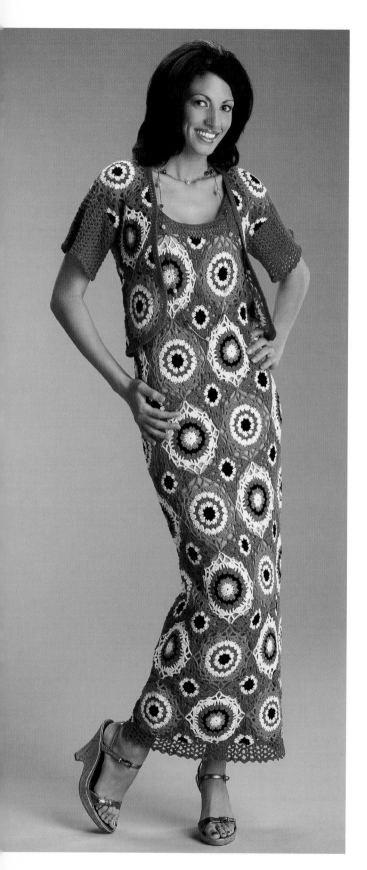

Rnd 3: Join in center st of any 3-st group, ch 3, 3 dc in next sc, [dc in center st of next 3-st group, 3 dc in next sc] 7 times, join, fasten off. *(32 dc)*

Rnd 4: Join in center st of any 3-st group, ch 3, 2 dc in same sp, sk next st, 5 dc in next st, [sk next st, 3 dc in next st, sk next st, 5 dc in next st] 7 times, join in 3rd ch of beg ch-3, fasten off. *(64 dc)*

Rnd 5: Join in center st of any 3-st group, ch 4, sk next st, dc in next st, sk next st, 5 dc in next st, sk next st, dc in next st, ch 1, sk next st, [dc in next st, ch 1, sk next st, sk next st, 5 dc in next st, sk next st, dc in next st, ch 1] 7 times, join in 3rd ch of beg ch-4. *(64 dc)*

Joining Rnd

First Strip
First Motif Only
Rnd 6: Ch 6 *(counts as first dc, ch-3)*, dc in same sp as joining, ch 2, (sc, ch 3, sc) in center st of next 5-st group, ch 2, sk next 3 sts, (tr, ch 5, tr) in next st, ch 2, (sc, ch 3, sc) in center st of next 5-st group, ch 2, sk next 3 sts, [(dc, ch 3, dc) in next st, ch 2, (sc, ch 3, sc) in center st of next 5-st group, ch 2, sk next 3 sts, (tr, ch 5, tr) in next st, ch 2, (sc, ch 3, sc) in center st of next 5-st group, ch 2, sk next 3 sts] 3 times, join in 3rd ch of beg ch-6, fasten off. *(16 sc, 8 dc, 8 tr)*

Motifs 2–7
Rnd 6: Ch 6 *(counts as first dc, ch-3)*, dc in same sp as joining, ch 2, (sc, ch 3, sc) in center st of next 5-st group, ch 2, sk next 3 sts, (tr, **ch-5 join**—*see Special Stitches*, tr) in next st, ch 2, (sc, ch 3, sc) in center st of next 5-st group, ch 2, sk next 3 sts, [(dc, ch 3, dc) in next st, ch 2, (sc, ch 3, sc) in center st of next 5-st group, ch 2, sk next 3 sts, (tr, ch 5, tr) in next st, ch 2, (sc, ch 3, sc) in center st of next 5-st group, ch 2, sk next 3 sts] 3 times, join in 3rd ch of beg ch-6, fasten off.

Strips 2–5
First Motif Only
Rnd 6: Rep rnd 6 of Motif 2.

Motifs 2–7
Rnd 6: Ch 6, dc in same sp as joining, ch 2, (sc, ch 3, sc) in center st of next 5-st group, ch 2, sk next 3 sts,

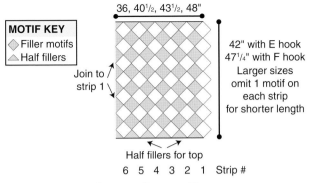

MOTIF KEY
◇ Filler motifs
△ Half fillers

36, 40½, 43½, 48"

42" with E hook
47¼" with F hook
Larger sizes
omit 1 motif on
each strip
for shorter length

Join to
strip 1

Half fillers for top

6 5 4 3 2 1   Strip #

Granny Square Dress
Joining Diagram

(tr, ch-5 join, tr) in next st, ch 2, (sc, ch 3, sc) in center st of next 5-st group, ch 2, sk next 3 sts, (dc, ch 3, dc) in next st, ch 2, (sc, ch 3, sc) in center st of next 5-st group, ch 2, sk next 3 sts, (tr, ch-5 join, tr) in next st, ch 2 (sc, ch 3, sc) in center st of next 5-st group, ch 2, sk next 3 sts, [(dc, ch 3, dc) in next st, ch 2, (sc, ch 3, sc) in center st of next 5-st group, ch 2, sk next 3 sts, (tr, ch 5, tr) in next st, ch 2, (sc, ch 3, sc) in center st of next 5-st group, ch 2, sk next 3 sts] twice, join in 3rd ch of beg ch-6, fasten off.

Strip 6
First Motif Only
Rnd 6: Joining this strip to corresponding Motif of both Strip 1 and Strip 5, ch 6, dc in same sp as joining, ch 2, (sc, ch 3, sc) in center st of next 5-st group, ch 2, sk next 3 sts, [(tr, ch-5 join, tr) in next st, ch 2, (sc, ch 3, sc) in center st of next 5-st group, ch 2, sk next 3 sts, (dc, ch 3, dc) in next st, ch 2, (sc, ch 3, sc) in center st of next 5-st group, ch 2, sk next 3 sts, (tr, ch 5, tr) in next st, ch 2, (sc, ch 3, sc) in center st of next 5-st group, ch 2, sk next 3 sts, (dc, ch 3, dc) in next st, ch 2, (sc, ch 3, sc) in center st of next 5-st group, ch 2, sk next 3 sts] twice, ch 2, (sc, ch 3, sc) in center st of next 5-st group, ch 2, sk next 3 sts, (dc, ch 3, dc) in next st, ch 2, (sc, ch 3, sc) in center st of next 5-st group, ch 2, join in 3rd ch of beg ch-6, fasten off.

Motifs 2–7
Rnd 6: Joining this strip to corresponding Motif of both Strip 1 and Strip 5, ch 6, dc in same sp as joining,

ch 2, (sc, ch 3, sc) in center st of next 5-st group, ch 2, sk next 3 sts, [(tr, ch-5 join, tr) in next st, ch 2, (sc, ch 3, sc) in center st of next 5-st group, ch 2, sk next 3 sts, (dc, ch 3, dc) in next st, ch 2, (sc, ch 3, sc) in center st of next 5-st group, ch 2, sk next 3 sts] 3 times, ch 2, (sc, ch 3, sc) in center st of next 5-st group, ch 2, sk next 3 sts, (dc, ch 3, dc) in next st, ch 2, (sc, ch 3, sc) in center st of next 5-st group, ch 2, join in 3rd ch of beg ch-6, fasten off.

Filler Motif

Rnd 1: With black, rep rnd 1 of Large Motif. *(16 dc)*

Rnd 2: Attach ecru with sc in any st, 3 dc in next st, [sc in next st, 3 dc in next st] 7 times, join in beg sc, fasten off. *(8 sc, 24 dc)*

Rnd 3: Attach terra cotta with sc in any sc, 2 sc in same st, sk next st, sc in next st, sk next st, (3 tr, ch 3, 3 tr) in next st, sk next st, sc in next st, sk next st, [3 sc in next st, sk next st, sc in next st, sk next st, (3 tr, ch 3, 3 tr) in next st, sk next st, sc in next st, sk next st] 3 times, join in beg sc. *(20 sc, 24 tr)*

Joining Rnd

Rnd 4: Working in openings between flower motifs, ch 3, drop lp, insert hook in center ch of corresponding ch-3 on flower motif, pick up dropped lp and draw through, ch 1, hdc in same st on filler motif, ch 2, sk next 3 sts, (hdc, **ch-3 join**—*see Special Stitches*, hdc) in next st, sk next st, (3 tr, ch-5 join, 3 tr) in next ch-3 sp, sk next st, (hdc, ch-3 join, hdc) in next st, ch 2, sk next 3 sts, [(hdc, ch-3 join, hdc) in next st, ch 2, sk next 3 sts, (hdc, ch-3 join, hdc) in next st, (3 tr, ch-5 join, 3 tr) in next ch-3 sp, sk next st, (hdc, ch-3 join, hdc) in next st, ch 2, sk next 3 sts] 3 times, join in 2nd ch of beg ch-3, fasten off. *(24 hdc, 24 tr)*

Half Filler For Top of Dress

Rnd 1: With black, ch 3, join in 3rd ch from hook to form a ring, ch 3, 8 dc in ring, fasten off. *(9 dc)*

Rnd 2: Join ecru with sc in first st, [3 dc in next st, sc in next st] 4 times, fasten off. *(5 sc, 12 dc)*

Rnd 3: Join terra cotta in first st, ch 3, 2 dc in same st, sk next st, sc in next st, sk next st, 3 sc in next st, sk next st, sc in next st, sk next st, (3 tr, ch 3, 3 tr) in next

st, sk next st, sc in next st, sk next st, 3 sc in next st, sk next st, sc in next st, sk next st, 3 dc in last st, turn. *(10 sc, 6 dc, 6 tr)*

Joining Rnd

Rnd 4: Working in openings along top and bottom, ch 5, drop lp, insert hook in center ch of corresponding ch-5 on Large Motif, pick up dropped lp and draw through, ch 2, dc in same sp on Half Filler, (hdc, ch-3 join, hdc) in next st, [ch 2, sk next 3 sts, (hdc, ch-3 join, hdc) in next st] twice, (3 tr, ch-5 join, 3 tr) in next ch-3 sp, sk next st, [(hdc, ch-3 join, hdc) in next st, ch 2, sk next 3 sts] twice, (hdc, ch-3 join, hdc) in next st, (dc, ch-5 join, dc) in last st, fasten off. *(12 hdc, 4 dc, 6 tr)*

Half Filler For Bottom of Dress

Rnds 1–3: Rep rnds 1–3 of Half Filler For Top of Dress.

Joining Rnd

Rnd 4: Working in openings along top and bottom, ch 6, drop lp, insert hook in center ch of corresponding ch-5 on Large Motif, pick up dropped lp and draw through, ch 2, tr in same sp on Half Filler, (hdc, ch-3 join, hdc) in next st, [ch 2, sk next 3 sts, (hdc, ch-3 join, hdc) in next st] twice, (3 tr, ch-5 join, 3 tr) in next ch-3 sp, sk next st, [(hdc, ch-3 join, hdc) in next st, ch 2, sk next 3 sts] twice, (hdc, ch-3 join, hdc) in next st, (tr, ch-5 join, tr) in last st, fasten off. *(12 hdc, 10 tr)*

Bottom Trim

Rnd 1: Join terra cotta in center ring of any Half Filler along bottom of Dress, ch 5, dc in same sp, working in row ends of Half Filler, [sk next row, (dc, ch 2, dc) in each of next 3 rows, (dc, ch 2, dc) in ch-5 sp on next Large Motif, (dc, ch 2, dc) in next 3 rows of next Half Filler, (dc, ch 2, dc) in center ring] around, omitting last (dc, ch 2, dc), join in 3rd ch of beg ch-5.

Rnds 2 & 3: Sl st in next ch-2 sp, ch 5, dc in same sp, (dc, ch 2, dc) in next ch-2 sp and each ch-2 sp to end, join in 3rd ch of beg ch-5.

Rnd 4: Sl st in next ch-2 sp, ch 1, (2 sc, ch 2, 2 sc) in same sp and each ch-2 sp to end, join in beg sc, fasten off.

Top Edging

Rnd 1: Join terra cotta in ch-5 sp of any Large Motif along top of dress, ch 3, 2 dc in same sp, working in row ends of Half Filler, [3 hdc in each of next 2 rows, hdc in each of next 2 rows, hdc in center of ring, hdc in each of next 2 rows, 3 hdc in each of next 2 rows, 3 dc in ch-5 sp on Large Motif] around, omitting last 3 dc, join in 3rd ch of beg ch-3. *(102 hdc, 18 dc)*

Front Panel

Row 1: Now working in rows, sl st in next st, ch 2 *(counts as first hdc)*, hdc in each of next 59 sts, turn. *(60 hdc)*

Row 2 & 3: Sl st in next st, ch 2, hdc in each st up to last st, leaving last st unworked, turn. *(56 hdc)*

Row 4: Sl st in next st, ch 2, hdc in each of next 18 sts, sc in each of next 18 sts, sc in each of next 18 sts, hdc in each of next 19 sts, turn. *(18 sc, 38 hdc)*

First Strap

Row 1: Ch 2, hdc in each of next 18 sts, turn. *(19 hdc)*

Row 2: Sl st in next st, ch 2, hdc in each st to end, turn. *(18 hdc)*

Row 3: Ch 2, hdc in each st to last st, leaving last st unworked, turn. *(17 hdc)*

Rows 4–11: [Rep rows 2 and 3 alternately] 4 times. *(9 hdc)*

Rows 12–22: Ch 2, hdc in each st to end, turn. At the end of last rep, fasten off.

2nd Strap

Row 1: Sk next 18 sts on Row 4 of Front Panel, join terra cotta in next st, ch 2, hdc in each of next 18 sts, turn.

Row 2: Ch 2, hdc in each st to last st, leaving last st unworked, turn.

Row 3: Sl st in next st, ch 2, hdc in each st to end, turn.

Rows 4–11: [Rep rows 2 and 3 alternately] 4 times.

Rows 12–22: Ch 2, hdc in each st to end, turn. At the end of last rep, fasten off.

Back Panel

Row 1: Join terra cotta in next st of Top Edging, ch 2, hdc in each of next 59 sts, turn. *(60 hdc)*

Rows 2–4: Rep rows 2–4 of Front Panel.

Straps

Rep pattern for Front Panel Straps.
Stitch last row of each Front Strap and Back Strap tog.

Collar Edging

Rnd 1: Join terra cotta with sc in first st of row 4 on Front Panel, sc in each of next 17 sts, working in row ends of First Strap, sc in each row, sc in each st across Back Panel, sc in each row end of 2nd Strap, join in beg sc, fasten off.

Armhole Trim

Rnd 1: Working in row ends of straps, around armhole opening, join terra cotta with sc in any row, sc in each row, join in beg sc.

Rnd 2: Ch 5, dc in same st, [sk next st, (dc, ch 2, dc) in

CONTINUED ON PAGE 46

SHAWL-COLLARED CARDIGAN

DESIGN BY MELISSA LEAPMAN

EASY

Finished Sizes

Instructions given fit 32–34-inch bust *(small)*; changes for 36–38-inch bust *(medium)*, 40–42-inch bust *(large)* and 44–46-inch bust *(X-large)* are in [ ].

Finished Garment Measurements

Bust: 37¾ inches *(small)* [40 inches *(medium)*, 43½ inches *(large)*, 46¾ inches *(X-large)*]
Length: 23½ inches *(small)* [24 inches *(medium)*, 24½ inches *(large)*, 25 inches *(X-large)*]

Gauge

14 sts = 4 inches; 12 rows = 4 inches
Take time to check gauge.

Special Stitches

Beginning increase (beg inc): (Ch 1, sc, dc) in sc or work (ch 3, sc) in dc.
End increase (end inc): (Sc, dc) in sc or (dc, sc) in dc.

MATERIALS

- Medium (worsted) weight yarn: 28 [32, 36, 40] oz/1,400 [1,600, 1,800, 2,000] yds/794 [907, 1,021, 1,134]g sapphire variegated
- Size H/8/5mm crochet hook or size needed to obtain gauge
- Tapestry needle
- Sewing needle
- Sewing thread
- 7 matching ¾-inch shank buttons
- Stitch markers

CARDIGAN

Back

Row 1 (RS): Beg at bottom, ch 66 [70, 76, 82], sc in 2nd ch from hook, [dc in next ch, sc in next ch] across, turn. *(65 [69, 75, 81] sts)*
Row 2: Ch 3 *(counts as first dc)*, [sc in next dc, dc in next sc] across, turn.
Row 3: Ch 1, [sc in next dc, dc in next sc] across, turn.
Rows 4–47: [Rep rows 2 and 3 alternately] 22 times.

Armhole Shaping

Row 48: Sl st in each of next 4 [6, 6, 8] sts, (sl st, ch 3) in next st, [sc in next dc, dc in next sc] across, leaving last 4 [6, 6, 8] sts unworked, turn. *(57 [57, 63, 65] sts)*
Row 49: Rep row 3.
Rows 50–71 [50–75, 50–75, 50–77]: [Rep rows 2 and 3 alternately] 11 [13, 13, 14] times.
Row 72 [76, 76, 78]: Rep row 2. Fasten off.

Pocket Lining
Make 2.
Row 1: Ch 18, sc in 2nd ch from hook, [dc in next ch, sc in next ch] across, turn. *(17 sts)*
Rows 2–17: [Rep rows 2 and 3 of Back] 8 times. At the end of last row, fasten off.

Left Front

Row 1 (RS): Ch 36 [38, 42, 44], sc in 2nd ch from hook, [dc in next ch, sc in next ch] across, turn. *(35 [37, 41, 43] sts)*

Rows 2–19: [Rep rows 2 and 3 of back alternately] 9 times.

Row 20 (WS): Ch 3, work as established across 7 [9, 11, 11] sts, pick up Pocket Lining and holding in place, work in pattern across 17 sts of Pocket Lining, sk next 17 sts of Left Front, work in pattern across rem 10 [10, 12, 14] sts, turn.

Row 21: Rep row 3 of Back.

Rows 22–47: [Rep rows 2 and 3 alternately of Back] 13 times.

Armhole Shaping

Row 48 (WS): Ch 3, work in pattern across leaving last 4 [6, 6, 8] sts unworked, turn. *(31 [31, 35, 35] sts)*

Rows 49 & 50 [49–52, 49–52, 49–54]: Rep rows 3 and 2 of Back alternately 1 [2, 2, 3] times.

Note: Place a marker at neckline edge, this will be the ending point of collar.

Neck Shaping

Row 1 (RS): Ch 1, work in pattern across to last 2 sts, **dc dec** *(see Stitch Guide)* in last 2 sts, turn. *(30 [30, 34, 34] sts)*

Row 2: Ch 1, sk first st, work in pattern across, turn. *(29 [29, 33, 33] sts)*

Rows 3–8: [Rep rows 1 and 2 of Neck Shaping] 3 times. *(23 [23, 27, 27] sts)*

Row 9: Ch 1, work in pattern across, turn.

Row 10: Ch 1, sk first st, work in pattern across row, turn. *(22 [22, 26, 26] sts)*

Rows 11–18 [11–18, 11–22, 11–22]: [Rep rows 9 and 10 alternately] 4 [4, 6, 6] times. *(18 [18, 20, 20] sts at end of last row)*

Rows 19–22 (19–24, 23 & 24, 23 & 24): Work in pattern across each row, turn. At the end of last row, fasten off.

Right Front

Rows 1 & 2: Rep rows 1 and 2 of Left Front.

Row 3: Ch 1, work first 2 sts in pattern, ch 2, sk next 2 sts *(buttonhole)*, work in pattern across, turn.

Row 4: Ch 3, work in pattern across, turn.

Row 5: Ch 1, work in pattern across, turn.

Rows 6–9: [Rep rows 4 and 5 alternately] twice.

Row 10: Rep row 4.

Rows 11–18: Rep rows 3–10.

Row 19: Rep row 3.

Row 20 (WS): Ch 3, work in pattern across 9 [9, 11, 13] sts, pick up Pocket Lining and holding in place, working in pattern across 17 sts of Pocket Lining, sk next 17 sts of Right Front, work in pattern across last 8 [10, 12, 12] sts, turn.

Rows 21–26: [Rep rows 5 and 4 alternately] 3 times.

Rows 27–42: [Rep rows 3–10 consecutively] twice.

Rows 43–47: Rep rows 3–7.

Armhole Shaping

Row 48: Sl st in each of first 4 [6, 6, 8] sts, [sl st, ch 3] in next st, work in pattern across, turn. *(31 [31, 35, 35] sts)*

Medium, Large & X-Large Sizes Only

Rows [49 & 50, 49 & 50, 49 & 50]: Rep rows 5 and 4.

All Sizes

Row 49 [51, 51, 51]: Rep row 3.

Row 50 [52, 52, 52]: Rep row 4.

X-Large Size Only

Rows 53 & 54: Rep rows 5 and 4.

Note: Place a marker at neckline edge, this will be the starting point of Collar.

Neck Shaping

Row 1: Ch 1, sk first st, work in pattern across, turn. *(30 [30, 34, 34] sts)*

Row 2: Ch 1, work in pattern across to last 2 sts, dc dec in last 2 sts, turn. *(29 [29, 33, 33] sts)*

Rows 3–8: Rep rows 1 and 2 alternately of Neck Shaping] twice. *(23 [23, 27, 27] sts at end of last row)*

Row 9: Ch 1, work in pattern across, turn.

Row 10: Ch 1, work in pattern across to last 2 sts, dc dec in last 2 sts, turn. *(22 [22, 26, 26] sts)*

Rows 11–18 [11–18, 11–22, 11–22]: [Rep rows 9 and 10 alternately] 4 [4, 6, 6] times. *(18 [18, 20, 20] sts at end of last row)*

Rows 19–22 [19–24, 23 & 24, 23 & 24]: Ch 1, work in pattern across row, turn. At the end of last row, fasten off.

Sleeve

Make 2.

Row 1 (RS): Ch 32 [32, 34, 36], rep row 1 of Back. *(31 [31, 33, 35] sts)*

Row 2: Ch 3, work in pattern across, turn.

Row 3: Ch 1, work in pattern across, turn.

Row 4 (WS): Beg inc *(see Special Stitches)*, work in pattern across row to last st, **end inc** *(see Special Stitches)* in last st, turn. *(33 [33, 35, 37] sts)*

Row 5: Ch 1, work in pattern across row, turn.

Rows 6 & 7 [6–9, 6–15, 6–19]: [Rep rows 4 and 5 alternately] 1 [2, 5, 7] times. *(35 [37, 45, 51] sts at end of last row)*

Rows 8–10 [10–12, 16–18, 20–22]: Rep rows 2, 3 and 2.

Row 11 [13, 19, 23]: Beg inc, work in pattern across row to last st, end inc in last st, turn. *(37 [39, 47, 53] sts)*

Next rows: Rep rows 8–11 [10–13, 16–19, 20–23] until there are 57 [63, 63, 69] sts.

Next rows: Rep rows 2 and 3 until Sleeve measures 20 inches or until Sleeve is desired length. At end of last row, fasten off.

Assembly

Sew each Pocket Lining to WS of Sweater.

Matching ends of rows of Back and Fronts tog, leaving center 21 [21, 23, 25] sts of Back unworked, sew each Front to Back across 18 [18, 20, 20] sts at each edge.

Matching center of last row of Sleeve to shoulder seam, sew last row of Sleeve to ends of rows on Front and Back to underarm, sew ends of rows at top of Sleeve to underarm on Front and Back. Sew Sleeve and side seams.

With sewing needle and thread, sew buttons on Left Front opposite buttonholes on Right Front.

Collar

Row 1: With RS facing, working around neckline edge, join with sl st at marker on Right Front, ch 1, sc in same st, evenly sp 30 [30, 32, 43] sc across to shoulder seam, sc in each of next 21 [21, 23, 25] sts across Back to next shoulder seam, evenly sp 31 [31, 33, 35] sc across to marked row on Left Front, turn. *(83 [83, 89, 95] sts)*

Row 2: Ch 1, sc dec in first 2 sts, dc in next st, [sc in next st, dc in next st] across to last 2 sts, sc dec in last 2 sts, turn. *(81 [81, 87, 93] sts)*

Rows 3–16: Ch 1, sc dec in first 2 sts, work in pattern across to last 2 sts, sc dec in last 2 sts, turn. *(53 [53, 59, 65] sts at end of last row)*

Rows 17–24: Ch 1, sc dec in first 3 sts, work in pattern across to last 3 sts, sc dec in last 3 sts, turn. At the end of last row, fasten off. *(21 [21, 27, 33] sts at end of last row)* ■

CROPPED BOMBER JACKET

DESIGN BY DARLA SIMS

INTERMEDIATE

Finished Sizes

Instructions given fit 32-34-inch bust *(small)*; changes for 36-38-inch bust *(medium)*, and 40-42-inch bust *(large)* are in [ ].

Finished Garment Measurements

Bust: 38½ inches *(small)* [44 inches *(medium)*, 49 inches *(large)*]

Gauge

Size G hook: 5 sc = 1 inch; 9 sc back lp rows = 2 inches
Size H hook: 10 hdc = 3 inches; 6 pattern rows = 2 inches
Take time to check gauge.

Pattern Note

Pattern is established in rows 4–9.

Special Stitches

Bobble: Hdc in each of next 5 sts, drop lp from hook, insert hook in first st of 5-hdc group, pull dropped lp through, push bobble to right side of work.

Cross-stitch (cross-st): Sk next 2 sts 3 rows below, working around last 2 rows, yo, insert hook in next st, yo, pull up long lp, yo, pull through all 3 lps on hook, sk next st

Materials

- Lion Brand Wool-Ease medium (worsted) weight yarn (3 oz/197 yds/85g per skein): 7 [8, 9] skeins #099 fisherman
- Sizes G/6/4mm and H/8/5mm crochet hooks or sizes needed to obtain gauge
- Tapestry needle
- Ornate hook and eyes: 5 sets

on last row behind st just made, hdc in next st on last row; working around last 2 rows, yo, insert hook in sk st 3 rows below, yo, pull up long lp, yo, pull through all 3 lps on hook, sk next st on last row behind st just made.

JACKET

Body

Row 1: With size H hook, ch 126 [142, 158], hdc in 3rd ch from hook *(2 sk chs count as first hdc)*, hdc in each ch across, turn. *(125 [141, 157] hdc)*

Row 2 (RS): Ch 2 *(counts as first hdc)*, hdc in each st across, turn.

Row 3: Ch 2, hdc in each st across, turn.

Row 4: Ch 2, hdc in each of next 3 sts, 5 hdc in next st, [hdc in each of next 3 sts, 5 hdc in next st] across to last 4 sts, hdc in each of last 4 sts, turn.

Row 5: Ch 2, hdc in each of next 3 sts, **bobble** *(see Special Stitches)*, [hdc in each of next 3 sts, bobble] across to last 4 sts, hdc in each of last 4 sts, turn.

Row 6: Ch 1, hdc in first st, **cross-st** *(see Special Stitches)*, [hdc in next bobble, cross-st] across to last st, hdc in last st, turn.

Rows 7–9: Ch 2, hdc in each st across, turn.

Rows 10–27: Work in pattern *(see Pattern Note)*.

Right Front

Row 28: Work in pattern across first 29 [33, 37] sts, hdc in next st, leave rem sts unworked, turn.

Rows 29–42: Work in pattern.

Neck Shaping

Row 43: Ch 2, hdc in each of next 23 [25, 28] sts, leave rem sts unworked, turn. *(24 [26, 29] hdc)*

Row 44: Ch 2, **hdc dec** *(see Stitch Guide)* in next 2 sts, work in pattern across, turn. *(23 [25, 28] hdc)*

Row 45: Work in pattern.

Rows 46–49: [Rep rows 44 and 45 alternately] twice. *(19, [21, 24] hdc at end of last row)*

Row 50: Rep row 44. *(20, [22, 25] hdc)*

Rows 51 [51, 51–53]: Ch 2, hdc in each st across, turn. At end of last row, fasten off.

Back

Row 28: Sk next st on row 27 *(armhole)*, join with sl st in next st, ch 2, 5 hdc in next st, [hdc in each of next 3 sts, 5 hdc in next st] 15 [17, 19] times, hdc in next st, leave rem sts unworked, turn. *(47 [53, 59] hdc, 16 [18, 20] hdc groups)*

Rows 29–48: Work in pattern.

Rows 49–51 [49–51, 49–53]: Ch 2, hdc in each st across, turn. At end of last row, fasten off.

Left Front

Row 28: Sk next st on row 27 *(armhole)*, join with sl st in next st, ch 2, 5 hdc in next st, [hdc in each of next 3 sts, 5 hdc in next st] 6 [7, 8] times, hdc in each of last 4 sts, turn.

Rows 29–42: Work in pattern. At end of last row, fasten off.

Neck Shaping

Rows 43: Sk first 6 [8, 9] sts, join with sl st in next st, ch 2, hdc in each st across, turn. *(24 [26, 29] hdc)*

Row 44: Work in pattern across to last 3 sts, hdc dec in next 2 sts, hdc in last st, turn. *(23 [25, 28] hdc)*

Row 45: Work in pattern.

Rows 46–49: [Rep rows 44 and 45 alternately] twice.

Row 50: Rep row 44. *(20 [22, 25] hdc)*

Rows 51 [51, 51–53]: Ch 2, hdc in each st across, turn. At end of last row, fasten off.

Sew shoulder seams.

Waist Ribbing

Row 1: Working in starting ch on opposite side of row 1 on Body, with size G hook, join with sc in first ch, sc in each of next 7 [3, 5] chs, **sc dec** *(see Stitch Guide)* in next 2 sts, [sc in each of next 4 chs, sc dec in next 2 sts] across to last 7 [3, 5] sts, sc in each of last 7 [3, 5] chs, turn. *(106 [118, 132] sc)*

Row 2: Ch 9, sc in 2nd ch from hook, sc in each ch across, sl st in each of first 2 sts on row 1, turn. *(8 sc)*

Row 3: Ch 1, sk sl sts, sc in **back lp** *(see Stitch Guide)* of each st across, turn.

Row 4: Ch 1, sc in back lp of each st across, sl st in both lps of each of next 2 sts on row 1, turn.

Rows 5–106 [5–118, 5–132]: [Rep rows 3 and 4 alternately] 51 [57, 64] times.

Row 107 [119, 133]: Rep row 3. Fasten off.

Right Front Placket

Row 1: Working in sts and in ends of rows across Right Front, with size G hook, join with sc in first st on Waist Ribbing, evenly sp 72 sc across to row 42 on Body, turn. *(73 sc)*

Row 2: Ch 6, sc in 2nd ch from hook, sc in each ch across, sl st in each of first 2 sts on row 1, turn. *(5 sc)*

Row 3: Working the following rows in back lps only, ch 1, sk sl sts, sc in each st across, turn.

Row 4: Ch 1, sc in back lp of each st across, sl st in each of next 2 sts on row 1, turn.

Rows 5–72: [Rep rows 3 and 4 alternately] 34 times.

Row 73: Rep row 3.

Row 74: Ch 1, sc in each st across, sl st in last st on row 1. Fasten off.

Left Front Placket

Row 1: Working in sts and in ends of rows across Left Front, with size G hook, join with sc in row 42, evenly sp 72 sc across, turn. *(73 sc)*

Rows 2–74: Rep same rows of Right Front Placket.

Neck Ribbing

Row 1: Working in sts and in ends of rows across neck edge, with size G hook, join with sc in first unworked st on row 42, evenly sp 69 sc across to last unworked st on row 42 on opposite side, turn. *(70 sc)*

Row 2: Ch 1, sl st in first st on row 1, ch 2, sc in 2nd ch from hook, sl st in each of next 2 sts on row 1, turn. *(1 sc)*

Row 3: Ch 1, sk sl sts, sc in back lp of next st, turn.

Row 4: Ch 2, sc in 2nd ch from hook, sc in back lp of next st, sl st in both lps of each of next 2 sts on row 1, turn. *(2 sc)*

Row 5: Ch 1, sk sl sts, sc in back lp of each st across, turn.

Row 6: Ch 2, sc in 2nd ch from hook, sc in back lp of

each st across, sl st in both lps of next 2 sts on row 1, turn. *(3 sc)*

Rows 7–10: Rep rows 5 and 6 alternately. *(5 sc at end of last row)*

Row 11: Ch 1, sk sl sts, sc in back lp of each st across, turn.

Row 12: Ch 1, sc in back lp of each st across, sl st in both lps of each of next 2 sts on row 1, turn.

Rows 13–62: [Rep rows 11 and 12 alternately] 25 times.

Row 63: Rep row 11.

Row 64: Ch 1, working in back lps, sc dec in first 2 sts, sc in each st across, sl st in both lps of each of next 2 sts on row 1, turn. *(4 sc)*

Row 65: Ch 1, sk sl sts, sc in back lp of each st across, turn.

Rows 66–69: [Rep rows 64 and 65 alternately] twice. *(2 sc at end of last row)*

Row 70: Ch 1, working in back lps, sc dec in first 2 sts, sl st in both lps of each of next 2 sts on row 1, turn. *(1 sc)*

Row 71: Ch 1, sk sl sts, sc in back lp of next st. Fasten off.

Sleeve

Make 2.

Row 1: With size H hook, ch 42, hdc in 3rd ch from hook, hdc in each ch across, turn. *(41 hdc)*

Rows 2 & 3: Ch 2, hdc in each st across, turn.

Row 4: Ch 2, hdc in each of next 3 sts, 5 hdc in next st, [hdc in each of next 3 sts, 5 hdc in next st] across to last 4 sts, hdc in each of last 4 sts, turn. *(32 hdc, 9 hdc groups)*

Row 5: For inc row, ch 2, hdc in same st, work in pattern across to last st, 2 hdc in last st, turn.

Note: *After working inc row, work next sts as needed to maintain pattern.*

Rows 6–8: Work in pattern.

Rows 9–36 [9–36, 9–44]: [Rep rows 5–8 consecutively] 14 [14, 18] times.

Row 37 [37, 45]: Rep row 5. *(59 [59, 63] hdc)*

Large Size Only

Fasten off.

Small & Medium Sizes Only

Rows 38–43 [38–45]: Work in pattern. At end of last row, fasten off.

For All Sizes

Matching center of last row on Sleeves to shoulder seams, sew Sleeves to armholes.

Sew hooks and eyes evenly spaced down Front Plackets as shown in photo. ■

RUBY GOES TO TOWN

DESIGN BY MARY BETH TEMPLE

INTERMEDIATE

Finished Sizes

Instructions given fit 32–34-inch bust *(small)*; changes for 36–38-inch bust *(medium)*, 40–42-inch bust *(large)*, 44–46-inch bust *(X-large)*, 48-50-inch bust *(2X-large)* and 52-54-inch bust *(3X-large)* are in [ ].

Finished Garment Measurements

Bust: 44 inches *(small)* [47 inches *(medium)*, 52 inches (large), 55 inches *(X-large)*, 60 inches *(2X-large)*, 64 inches *(3X-large)*]

Gauge

16 dc = 4 inches; 4 rows = 2 inches

Pattern Notes

Weave in loose ends as work progresses.
Garment is sized for a loose fit. For a closer fitting garment, go down one size.

WRAP

Back

Row 1 (RS): With A, ch 45 [47, 47, 47, 49, 49], dc in 4th ch from hook and in each rem ch across, turn.

Materials

- Bernat Cool Crochet light (DK) weight yarn (1¾ oz/200 yds/50g per ball):
  5 balls #74435 velveteen *(A)*
- Patons Grace light (DK) weight yarn (1¾ oz/136 yds/50g per ball):
  2 balls #60040 night *(B)*
- Size H/8/5mm crochet hook or size needed to obtain gauge
- Tapestry needle
- Straight pins

(42 [44, 44, 44, 46, 46] dc)
Row 2: Ch 3 *(counts as first dc)*, dc in each st across, turn.
Row 3: Ch 3, dc in each st across, ch 41 [43, 43, 43, 45, 45], turn.
Row 4: Dc in 4th ch from hook, dc in each ch and each dc across, turn. *(80 [84, 84, 84, 88, 88] dc)*
Row 5: Ch 3, dc in each st across, turn.
Rep row 5 until Back measures 21 [21½, 25, 26½, 29, 31] inches, ending with a RS row.
Row 6: Ch 3 *(counts as first dc)*, dc in each of next 41 [43, 43, 43, 45, 45] dc, turn. *(42 [44, 44, 44, 46, 46] dc)*
Rows 7 & 8: Rep row 6. At the end of row 8, fasten off.

Front
Make 2.
Row 1: With A, ch 83 [87, 87, 87, 91, 91], dc in 4th ch from hook, dc in each rem ch across, turn. *(80 [84, 84, 84, 88, 88] dc)*
Row 2: Ch 3, dc in each st across, turn.
Rep row 2 until Front measures 19 [20½, 23, 24½, 27, 29] inches.
Rows 3–5: Ch 3, dc in each dc across, turn. At the end of last rep, fasten off.
With RS facing, pin Fronts and Back tog and join shoulder seams with sc. Sc side seams tog, turn garment RS out.

Front Trim

Row 1: With RS facing, attach B at bottom of right front, ch 3, **fpdtr** *(see Stitch Guide)* around dc 2 rows below, sk dc directly behind fpdtr, [dc in each of next 3 dc, fpdtr around dc 2 rows below, sk dc directly behind fpdtr] up front, around neckline and down left front, ending with dc in last st, turn.

CONTINUED ON PAGE 47

PERFECT IN PLUM COAT

DESIGN PROVIDED COURTESY OF DMC CORPORATION

EXPERIENCED

Finished Size

Instructions given fit medium
  36–38-inch bust *(medium)*

Finished Garment Measurements

Bust: 43½ inches

Back Waist Length: 59 inches

Gauge

Motif: 6½ inches square; **Pattern Stitches 1, 2 and 3:** 19 sts = 5 inches; **Pattern Stitch 1:** 9 rows = 4 inches; **Pattern Stitch 2:** 9 rows = 4 inches; **Pattern Stitch 3:** 14 rows = 6 inches; **Pattern Stitch 4:** 4 rows = 3 inches

Pattern Notes

Weave in loose ends as work progresses.

Hold 2 strands of crochet cotton together as 1 throughout unless otherwise stated.

Join rounds with slip stitch unless otherwise stated.

Special Stitches

Bobble: [Yo, insert hook in indicated st, yo, draw up a lp, yo, draw through 2 lps on hook] 5 times in indicated st, yo, draw through all 6 lps on hook, ch 1 to lock.

Shell: 3 dc in indicated st.

Pattern Stitch 1

Row 1 (WS): Ch 3 *(counts as first dc)*, **bpdc** *(see Stitch Guide)* around next st, [**fpdc**—*see Stitch Guide)* around

Materials

- DMC Senso Wool Cotton size 3 crochet cotton (100 yds per ball):
    69 balls #1308 plum
- Size H/8/5mm crochet hook or size needed to obtain gauge
- Tapestry needle
- Stitch markers
- 1¼-inch wooden buttons: 6

each of next 2 sts, bpdc around each of next 2 sts] across, ending with bpdc around next st, dc in last st, turn.

Row 2: Ch 3, fpdc around next st, [bpdc around each of next 2 sts, fpdc around each of next 2 sts] across, ending with fpdc around next st, dc in last st, turn.

Pattern Stitch 2

Row 1 (WS): Ch 1, sc in each st across, turn.

Row 2: Ch 3, dc in each of next 2 sts, [**bobble** *(see Special Stitches)* in next st, dc in each of next 3 sts] across, turn.

Row 3: Rep row 1.

Row 4: Ch 3, dc in next st, [ch 2, sk next 2 sts, dc in each of next 2 sts] across, turn.

Row 5: Ch 3, fpdc around next st, [dc in each of next 2 chs, fpdc around each of next 2 sts] across, turn.

Row 6: Rep row 4.

Row 7: Rep row 1.

Row 8: Rep row 2.

Row 9: Rep row 1.

Pattern Stitch 3

Row 1 (WS): Ch 3, bpdc around next st, [fpdc around each of next 6 sts, bpdc around each of next 2 sts] across, ending with bpdc around next st, dc in last st, turn.

Row 2: Ch 3, fpdc around next st, [bpdc around each of next 2 sts, fpdc around each of next 2 sts] across, ending with fpdc around next st, dc in last st, turn.

Row 3: Ch 3, bpdc around next st, [fpdc around each of next 2 sts, bpdc around each of next 2 sts] across, ending with bpdc in next st, dc in last st, turn.

Row 4: Ch 3, fpdc around next st, [bpdc around each of

CONTINUED ON PAGE 48

CONFETTI COVER-UP

DESIGN BY LISA GONZALEZ

EASY

Finished Sizes

Instructions given fit woman's small/medium; changes for medium/large, large/X-large, 2X-large and 3X-large are in [ ].

Finished Garment Measurements

Bust: 34–36 inches *(small/medium)* [38–40-inches *(medium/large)*, 42–46 inches *(large/X-large)*, 48–50 inches *(2X-large)*, 52–54 inches *(3X-large)*]

Materials

- Classic Elite Bangles bulky (chunky) weight yarn (1¾ oz/83 yds/50g per ball): 24 [25, 25, 26, 27] balls #6704 heliotrope
- Size K/10½/6.5mm crochet hook or size needed to obtain gauge
- Blunt-end yarn needle
- Stitch markers

Gauge

[Dc, ch 1] 6 times = 4 inches; 6 rows = 4 inches

Pattern Notes

Weave in loose ends as work progresses.
Join rounds with a slip stitch unless otherwise stated.
Cover-up is crocheted vertically in several pieces then assembled.
Pattern also includes a cropped version of the Cover-up following each piece.

COVER-UP

Back

Row 1: Loosely ch 117 [123, 129, 135, 135], dc in 5th ch from hook, [ch 1, sk 1 ch, dc in next ch] across, ending with dc in last ch, turn.

Row 2: Ch 4 *(counts as first dc, ch-1)*, sk first dc, [dc in next ch-1 sp, ch 1, sk next dc] across, ending with dc in last ch sp, turn. *(113 [119, 125, 131, 131] sts)*
Rep row 2 until Back measures 20 [23, 25, 27, 29] inches wide when placed on a flat surface, fasten off.

Cropped Back

Row 1: Ch 54 [59, 65, 71, 71], rep row 1 of Back.
Row 2: Rep row 2 of Back. *(49 [55, 61, 67, 67] sts)*
Rep row 2 until Cropped Back measures the same width as Back.

Front

Make 2.
Row 1: Rep row 1 of Back.
Row 2: Rep row 2 of Back.
Rep row 2 until Front measures 8 [9, 10, 11, 12] inches wide when placed on a flat surface.

Cropped Front

Make 2.
Row 1: Ch 54 [59, 65, 71, 71], rep row 1 of Front.
Row 2: Rep row 2 of Front.
Rep row 2 until Cropped Front measures the same width as Front.

Neckline Shaping

Row 3: Ch 4, sk first dc, *dc in ch-1 sp, sk next dc, ch 1, rep from * for 93 [99, 105, 109, 109] sts, leaving rem sts unworked, turn.
Row 4: Ch 4, sk first dc, [dc in next ch-1 sp, ch 1, sk next dc] across, ending with dc in last ch sp, turn.
Rep row 4 until Front measures 10 [11½, 12½, 13½, 14½] inches wide when placed on a flat surface, fasten off.

Cropped Neckline Shaping

Row 3: Ch 4, sk next dc, *dc in ch-1 sp, sk next dc, ch 1, rep from * for 29 [35, 41, 45, 45] sts, leaving rem sts unworked, turn.
Row 4: Ch 4, sk first dc, [dc in next ch-1 sp, ch 1, sk next dc] across, ending with dc in last ch sp, turn.
Rep row 4 until Cropped Neckline Shaping measures the same width as Neckline Shaping. Fasten off.

Sleeve

Make 2.

Row 1: Ch 61 [63, 63, 65, 65], dc in 5th ch from hook, [ch 1, sk 1 ch, dc in next ch] across, turn.

Row 2: Ch 4, sk first dc, [dc in next ch-1 sp, ch 1, sk next dc] across, ending with dc in last ch sp, turn.

Rep row 2 until Sleeve measures 14½ [15, 16, 17, 18] inches when placed on a flat surface, fasten off. Holding sides of Sleeve tog, sew or crochet tog.

Cropped Sleeve

Make 2.

Row 1: Ch 23 [25, 25, 27, 27], rep row 1 of Sleeve starting with dc in 5th ch.

Row 2: Rep row 2 of Sleeve.

Rep row 2 until cropped Sleeve measures the same width as Sleeve. Holding sides of Sleeve tog, sew or crochet tog.

Assembly

Sew or crochet Fronts and Back tog at shoulders. Center Sleeve at shoulder seam, sew or crochet Sleeve into armhole opening. Sew or crochet side seams tog, leaving approximately 5 inches unattached at each bottom side seam.

Cover-up Edging

Rnd 1: Beg at back neck, loosely sc around, taking care to sc in ch-1 sps only. Work 3 sc in each front neckline corner, bottom front and side corners, join in beg sc, fasten off.

Sleeve Edging

Rnd 1: Beg at Sleeve seam, sc around taking care to sc in ch-1 sps only, join in beg sc, fasten off.

Finishing

Taking care not to twist ribbon, weave ribbon through ch-1 sps on row just below bust, tie ends in a bow. ■

GRANNY SQUARE DRESS & JACKET CONTINUED FROM PAGE 29

next st] around, join in 3rd ch of beg ch-5, fasten off. Rep on other armhole.

JACKET

Strip 1

First Motif

Rnds 1–6: Rep Large Motif for Dress.

Motifs 2–5

Rep Large Motif for Dress.

Motif 6

Rnds 1–5: Rep rnds 1-5 of Large Motif for Dress.

Rnd 6: Folding strip in half and joining to First Motif to create side seam, ch 6, dc in same sp as joining, ch 2, (sc, ch 3, sc) in center st of next 5-st group, ch 2, sk next 3 sts, (tr, ch-5 join, tr) in next st, joining to First Motif, ch 2, (sc, ch 3, sc) in center st of next 5-st group, ch 2, sk next 3 sts, (tr, ch-5 join, tr) in next st, joining to Motif 5 of current strip, ch 2, (sc, ch 3, sc) in center st of next 5-st group, ch 2, sk next 3 sts, (dc, ch 3, dc) in next st, ch 2, (sc, ch 3, sc) in center st of next 5-st group, ch 2, sk next 3 sts, (tr, ch 5, tr) in next st, ch 2, (sc, ch 3, sc) in center st of next 5-st group, ch 2, sk next 3 sts, (dc, ch 3, dc) in next st, ch 2, (sc, ch 3, sc) in center of next 5-st group, ch 2, sk next 3 sts, (tr, ch 5, tr) in next st, ch 2, (sc, ch 3, sc) in center of next 5-st group, ch 2, join in 3rd ch of beg ch-6, fasten off.

Strip 2

First Motif

Rnds 1–6: Rep Large Motif for Dress.

Motifs 2 & 3

Rep Large Motif for Dress.

Strip 3

First Motif

Rnds 1–6: Rep Large Motif for Dress.

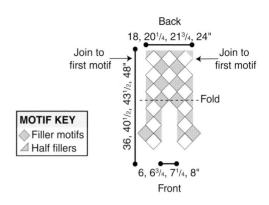

**Granny Square Jacket
Joining Diagram**

Motifs 2–5

Rep Large Motif for Dress.

Motif 6

Rnds 1–5: Rep rnds 1-5 of Large Motif for Dress.

Rnd 6: Rep rnd 6 of Motif 6 of Jacket.

Filler Motif

Using diagram as a guide, rep rnds 1-4 of Filler Motif for Dress.

Half Filler Motif

Using diagram as a guide, rep rnds 1-4 of Half Filler Motif for Top of Dress.

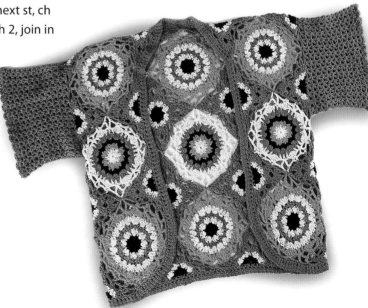

Sleeve

Rnd 1: Working in row ends of Half Fillers around armhole opening, join terra cotta in center of side seam, [3 sc in next row, 2 sc in next row, sc in next row, 2 sc in next row, sc in bottom of ring, 2 sc in next row, sc in next row, 2 sc in next row, 3 sc in next row, sc in ch-5 sp on next Large Motif] 3 times, omitting last sc, sk sl st, join in first sc. *(54 sc)*

Rnd 2: Ch 4, dc in same st, sk next st, [**V-st** *(see Special Stitches)* in next st, sk next st] around, join in 3rd ch of beg ch-4. *(27 V-sts)*
Rep on opposite Armhole.

Rnds 3–12: Sl st into first ch-1 sp, ch 4, dc in same ch-1 sp, V-st in ch-1 sp of each V-st around, join in 3rd ch of beg ch-4.

Rnd 13: Sl st into first ch-1 sp, ch 3, 2 dc in same sp, sl st in sp before next V-st, [3 dc in next V-st, sl st in sp before next V-st] around, join in 3rd ch of beg ch-3, fasten off.

Front Panel & Neck Edging

Rnd 1: Starting at bottom of right front panel, join terra cotta with sc in center ch-5 sp on Large Motif, 3 sc in same sp, 3 sc in next ch-2 sp, 2 sc in next ch-3 sp, 3 sc in next ch-2 sp, 4 sc in next ch-3 sp, 3 sc in next ch-2 sp, 2 sc in next ch-3 sp, 3 sc in next ch-2 sp, 3 sc in next ch-5 sp, working in row ends of Half Fillers, *3 sc in next row, 2 sc in next row, sc in next row, 2 sc in next row, sc in bottom of ring, 2 sc in next row, sc in next row, 2 sc in next row, 3 sc in next row, sc in ch-5 sp on next Large Motif*, rep between * twice, working in sps and sts of Filler Motifs along back of neck, 3 sc in next ch-3 sp, [sc in each of next 4 sts, (sc in next ch-3 sp, sc in next st, 2 sc in next ch-2 sp, sc in next st) twice, sc in next ch-3 sp, sc in each of next 4 sts, sc in ch-5 sp on next Large Motif] twice, rep between * twice, 3 sc in next ch-5 sp, 3 sc in next ch-2 sp, 2 sc in next ch-3 sp, 3 sc in next ch-2 sp, 4 sc in next ch-3 sp, 3 sc in next ch-2 sp, 2 sc in next ch-3 sp, 3 sc in next ch-2 sp, 4 sc in next ch-5 sp, working along bottom of back, rep between * 3 times, 3 sc in next row, 2 sc in next row, sc in next row, 3 sc in next row, join in beg sc.

Rnd 2: Ch 3, dc in each st around, join in 3rd ch of beg ch-3.

Rnd 3: Ch 1, sc in first st, ch 1, [sc in next st, ch 1] around, join in beg sc, fasten off. ■

RUBY GOES TO TOWN CONTINUED FROM PAGE 39

CONTINUED FROM PAGE 39

Row 2: Ch 4, sk fpdtr, [dc in each of next 3 dc, ch 1, sk fpdtr] across, ending with dc in last dc, turn.

Row 3: Ch 1, sc in first dc, (hdc, dc, tr, dc, hdc) in ch-1 sp, [sc in each of next 3 dc, (hdc, dc, tr, dc, hdc) in next ch-1 sp] across, ending with sc in last dc, fasten off.

Arm Trim

Row 1: With RS facing, attach B at back of armhole for right Arm Trim *(at front of armhole for left Arm Trim)* *(do not work row 1 in ends of rows at underarm)*, ch 3, *fpdtr around vertical post of dc 2 rows below, sk dc directly behind fpdtr**, dc in each of next 3 dc, rep from * around armhole to opposite edge, ending last rep at **, dc in next dc, turn.

Row 2: Ch 3, sk 1 unworked row to the left toward underarm, sl st in side edge of 2nd dc row at underarm, ch 1, *dc in each of next 3 dc, ch 1, sk next fpdtr**, rep from * around armhole, ending last rep at **, sk next row of underarm, sl st in next row, turn.

Row 3: Ch 1, sc in first dc, (hdc, dc, tr, dc, hdc) in ch-1 sp, [sc in each of next 3 dc, (hdc, dc, tr, dc, hdc) in next ch-1 sp] across, ending with sc in last dc, fasten off. Rep on opposite armhole. ■

PERFECT IN PLUM COAT CONTINUED FROM PAGE 40

next 6 sts, fpdc around each of next 2 sts] across, ending with fpdc around next st, dc in last st, turn.

Row 5: Rep row 3.

Row 6: Rep row 2.

Row 7: Rep row 1.

Row 8: Ch 3, bpdc around each of next 3 sts, [fpdc around each of next 2 sts, bpdc around each of next 6 sts] across, ending with bpdc around each of next 3 sts, dc in last st, turn.

Row 9: Rep row 3.

Row 10: Rep row 2.

Row 11: Ch 3, fpdc around each of next 3 sts, [bpdc around each of next 2 sts, fpdc around each of next 6 sts] across, ending with fpdc around each of next 3 sts, dc in last st, turn.

Row 12: Rep row 2.

Row 13: Rep row 3.

Row 14: Rep row 8.

Pattern Stitch 4

Row 1 (WS): Ch 3, [sk next 2 sts, **shell** (*see Special Stitches*) in next st, shell in previous st] across, ending with sk 2 dc in last st where applicable, turn.

Row 2: Ch 4, shell in same st, [sk next shell, shell in first dc of next shell, shell in last dc of previous shell] across, 4 dc in last st, turn.

Row 3: Ch 3, [shell in first dc of next shell, shell in last dc of previous shell] across, dc in last st, turn.

COAT

Back

Row 1: Ch 84, dc in 4th ch from hook (*first 3 chs count as first dc*), dc in each rem ch across, turn. (*82 dc*)

Row 2: Working Pattern Stitch 1, work row 1.

Rows 3–19: Working Pattern Stitch 1, rep row 2.

Rows 20–28: Work Pattern Stitch 2.

Row 29: Ch 3, dc in each st across, turn.

Rows 30–92: Work Pattern Stitch 3 [rows 1–14] 4 times, rep rows 1–7.

Armhole

Row 93: Sl st in each of first 12 sts, ch 4, work row 1 of Pattern Stitch 4 in next 60 sts, leaving rem sts un-worked, turn.

Row 94: Work row 1 of Pattern Stitch 4.

Row 95: Work row 2 of Pattern Stitch 4.

Row 96: Work row 3 of Pattern Stitch 4.

Rows 97–104: Rep rows 2 and 3 of Pattern Stitch 4. At end of last row, fasten off.

Front

Make 2.

Row 1: Ch 44, dc in 4th ch from hook (*3 sk chs count as first dc*), dc in each rem ch across, turn. (*42 dc*)

Rows 2–92: Rep rows 2–92 of Back.

Left Armhole

Row 93: Sl st in each of first 12 sts, ch 3, work row 1 of Pattern Stitch 4 in each st across, turn.

Right Armhole

Row 93: Ch 3, work row 1 of Pattern Stitch 4 in each st across, leaving last 11 sts unworked, turn.

Left & Right Front

Rows 94–104: Rep rows 94–104 of Back.

Sleeve

Make 2.

Row 1: Ch 48, dc in 4th ch from hook (*3 sk chs count as first dc*), dc in each rem ch across, turn. (*46 dc*)

Rows 2–43: Rep rows 2–43 of Back, inc 1 st at beg and end of every 4th row. (*66 sts*)

Rows 44–50: Work rows 1–7 of Pattern Stitch 2. At the end of last row, fasten off.

Motif

Make 7.

Rnd 1: Ch 10, sl st in first ch to form ring, ch 1, 16 sc in ring, join in beg sc. (*16 sc*)

Rnd 2: Ch 7 (*counts as first dc, ch-4*), sk next st, [dc in next st, ch 4, sk next st] around, join in 3rd ch of beg ch-7.

Rnd 3: Sl st in next ch sp, ch 1, (sc, dc, tr, ch 1, tr, dc, sc) in same ch sp, (sc, dc, tr, ch 1, tr, dc, sc) in each ch sp around, join in beg sc.

Rnd 4: Ch 9 (*counts as first tr, ch-5*), *[sc in next ch-1 sp, ch 5] twice, tr in sp between next 2 sts, ch 5, rep from * around, ending with ch 5, sl st in 4th ch of beg ch-9.

Rnd 5: Ch 4, *[dc in each of next 5 chs, sk next st] twice, dc in each of next 5 chs, (tr, ch 3, tr) in next tr, rep from * around, ending with ch 3, sl st in 4th ch of beg ch-4.

Rnd 6: Ch 1, *sc in each of first 15 dc, sc in next tr, sc in next ch, ch 1, sk next ch, sc in next ch, sc in next tr, rep from * around, ending with last sc in 4th ch of beg ch-4 of previous rnd, fasten off.

Border

Working in ends of rows, join with sc in bottom corner of 1 Front, evenly sp sc across, fasten off. Rep Border on rem front.

Right Front Only

Join with sc at the end of Pattern Stitch 2, *sc in next st, hdc in each of next 2 sts, dc in each of next 2 sts, tr in next st, ch 1 (*buttonhole*), tr in next st, dc in each of next 2 sts, hdc in each of next 2 sts, sc in next st, rep from * across to end of Pattern Stitch 3, fasten off.

Assembly

With RS tog, sc shoulder seams tog across 4½ inches. Fold first Sleeve in half, place fold at shoulder seam, sc in place, fasten off. Attach 2nd Sleeve in same manner. With RS tog, sc Sleeve and side seams closed.

Sew buttons to Left Front opposite ch-1 buttonhole sps of Right Front.

Sew 3 Motifs in diamond shape to Back and 1 to each Front and each Sleeve. ∎

WRAPS

Wraps add the perfect finishing touch to a variety of styles from daytime chic to nighttime glamour. From simple to sophisticated, our charming collection of shawls, shrugs and ponchos will have you covered for any occasion.

GOLD NUGGET COCKTAIL COVER-UP

DESIGN BY LAINIE HERING

INTERMEDIATE

Finished Size

One size fits most

Gauge

Squares = 8 inches square

Special Stitches

Beginning Popcorn (beg pc): Ch 4 *(counts as first tr)*, 3 tr in same ch sp, drop lp from hook, insert hook in top of beg ch-4, pull dropped lp through.

Popcorn (pc): 4 tr in ch sp indicated, drop lp from hook, insert hook in first tr of group, pull dropped lp through.

Materials

- Plymouth 24K light (DK) weight yarn (4 oz/187 yds/113g per ball) :
    3 balls #61 gold
- Plymouth Eros novelty weight nylon ladder yarn (2 oz/165 yds/57g per ball) :
    1 ball #3253 gold
- Size H/8/5mm crochet hook or size needed to obtain gauge
- Tapestry needle

3 LIGHT

COVER-UP

Square
Make 6.
Rnd 1: With 24K, ch 5, sl st in first ch to form ring, **beg pc** *(see Special Stitches)* in ring, ch 3, [**pc** *(see Special Stitches)* in ring, ch 3] 3 times, join with sl st in top of beg pc. *(4 pc, 4 ch sps)*

Rnd 2: Sl st in first ch sp, ch 4 *(counts as first tr)*, 2 tr, ch 3, 3 tr) in same ch sp, ch 1, *(3 tr, ch 3, 3 tr) in next ch sp, ch 1, rep from * around, join with sl st in top of ch-4. *(24 tr, 4 ch-1 sps, 4 ch-3 sps)*

Rnd 3: Sl st in each of next 2 sts, sl st in next ch-3 sp, ch 4, (2 tr, ch 3, 3 tr) in same ch-3 sp, ch 2, 3 tr in next ch-1 sp, ch 2, *(3 tr, ch 3, 3 tr) in next ch-3 sp, ch 2, 3 tr in next ch-1 sp, ch 2, rep from * around, join with sl st in 4th ch of beg ch-4. *(36 tr, 8 ch-2 sps, 4 ch-3 sps)*

Rnds 4–6: Sl st in each of next 2 sts, sl st in next ch-3 sp, ch 4, (2 tr, ch 3, 3 tr) in same ch-3 sp, ch 2, [3 tr in next ch-2 sp, ch 2] across to next corner ch-3 sp, *(3 tr, ch 3, 3 tr) in next ch-3 sp, ch 2, [3 tr in next ch-2 sp, ch 2] across to next corner ch-3 sp, rep from * around, join with sl st in 4th ch of beg ch-4. At end of last rnd, fasten off. *(72 tr, 20 ch-2 sps, 4 ch-3 sps)*

Shoulder Piece
Make 4.
Join 24K with sl st in any corner ch sp, ch 4, evenly sp 24 tr across to next corner ch sp. Fasten off.

CONTINUED ON PAGE 79

ENCHANTED EVENING

DESIGN BY LAURA GEBHARDT

EASY

Finished Sizes

Instructions given fit small; changes medium, large, X-large and 2X-large are in [ ].

Materials

- SRK Collection Sari bulky (chunky) weight nylon ribbon (1¾ oz/104 yds/50g per ball):
  5 [6, 7, 8, 8] balls #58 pink
- Size K/10½/6.5mm crochet hook or size needed to obtain gauge
- Tapestry needle

Gauge

12 sc = 4 inches; 13 sc rows = 4 inches

Pattern Note

Weave in loose ends as work progresses.

Special Stitches

Paris stitch (Paris st): (2 dc, ch 2, sc) in indicated st or sp.
Beginning Paris stitch (beg Paris st): Ch 3 *(counts as first dc)*, (dc, ch 2, sc) in same st as beg ch-3.

CAPELET

Collar

Row 1: Ch 98 [102, 106, 110, 114], sc in 2nd ch from hook, sc in each rem ch across, turn. *(97 [101, 105, 109, 113] sc)*
Row 2: Ch 1, sc in each sc across, turn.
Rows 3–12 [3–12, 3–14, 3–15, 3–15]: Rep row 2.

For Sizes X-Large & 2X-Large Only
Row 16: Ch 1, 2 sc in first sc, sc in each sc to approximate halfway point of row, 2 sc in each of next 2 sc, sc in each rem sc to last sc, 2 sc in last sc, turn. ([113, 117] sc)

Body

For All Sizes
Row 13 [13, 15, 17, 17]: Beg Paris st (see Special Stitches) in first st, [sk next st, **Paris st** (see Special Stitches) in next st] across, turn. (49 [51, 53, 57, 59] Paris sts)
Rows 14–37 [14–37, 16–43, 18–49, 18–49]: Beg Paris st in first ch-2 sp, [Paris st in each rem ch-2 sp] across, turn.

Ties

Row 1: With RS facing, attach yarn with sl st in sc at end of row 12 [12, 14, 16, 16], ch 80, sl st in 2nd ch from hook, sl st in each rem ch across, fasten off.
Rep row 1 of Ties on opposite side of row 12 [12, 14, 16, 16].

Collar Edging

Row 1: With RS facing, working in opposite side of foundation ch, attach yarn, ch 1, **reverse sc** (see Fig. 1) in each ch across, leaving a length, fasten off.
Thread rem length into tapestry needle, fold Collar in half and tack beg and end of Collar and loose edge of Collar as desired. ■

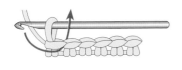
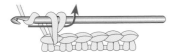

**Reverse Single Crochet
Fig. 1**

BUTTERFLIES & ROSES FILET SHAWL

DESIGN BY KATHRYN WHITE

INTERMEDIATE

Finished Size

30 x 84 inches

Gauge

9 extended dc = 1 inch; 7 extended dc rows = 2 inches

Pattern Notes

Weave in loose ends as work progresses.

It is recommended to check design after every row for accuracy to avoid missing or adding blocks or mesh and having to redo sections

Chart shows half the Shawl. Follow chart to center, then from center back out to edge.

Special Stitches

Extended double crochet (extended dc): Yo, insert hook in indicated st, yo, draw up lp, [yo, draw through 2 lps on hook] twice.

Mesh: (Extended dc in next st, ch 2, sk next 2 sts,

Materials

- Grandma's Best size 10 crochet cotton (350 yds per ball):
    7 balls cream
- Sewing thread (1,000 yds per spool):
    3 spools gold
- Size 5/1.90mm steel crochet hook or size needed to obtain gauge
- Big-eye beading needle
- Size 8 gold seed beads: 85g

extended dc in next st) for 1 mesh. When 1 or more mesh are side by side, they share the center st between them, so 2 meshes will be (extended dc in next st, ch 2, sk next 2 sts) twice and extended dc in next st.

Block: 4 extended dc make up 1 block. When one or more blocks are side by side, they share the center st between them, so 2 blocks will be 7 extended dc, 3 blocks will be 10 extended dc and 4 blocks will be 13 extended dc.

Increase a block at beginning of row (inc a block at beg of row): Ch 5, extended dc in 4th ch from hook, extended dc in next ch, extended dc in next extended dc.

Increase multiple blocks at beginning of row (inc multiple blocks at beg of row): Ch 5 for first inc and add 3 more chs for each block required. For 2 block inc, ch 8; 3 block inc, ch 11; 4 block inc, ch 14; 5 block inc, ch 17; 6 block inc, ch 20; extended dc in 4th ch from hook and in each rem ch.

Increase a block or blocks at end of row (inc a block or blocks at end of row): For first extended dc, tr in the base of the last extended dc where it joins the row, work a tr in the base of the previous tr just completed, continue adding sts in this manner until the required number of blocks is completed. For each block, add 3 sts as the last extended dc of the row counts as the shared st. For 2 blocks, 6 tr; 3 blocks, 9 tr; 4 blocks, 12 tr; 5 blocks, 15 tr; 6 blocks, 18 tr.

Decrease at beginning of row (dec at beg of row): Sl st across the top of the number of meshes or blocks required to complete the next extended dc, then (ch

5, sk next 2 sts, extended dc in next extended dc) for mesh st or (ch 3, extended dc in next 3 sts) for block.

Decrease at end of row (dec at end of row): Work indicated number of blocks or mesh required as indicated by chart.

Bead single crochet (bead sc): Insert hook in indicated st, yo, draw up a lp, move 1 bead up next to work, yo, draw through 2 lps on hook.

3-bead single crochet (3-bead sc): Insert hook in indicated st, yo, draw up a lp, move 3 beads up next to work, yo, draw through 2 lps on hook.

4-bead single crochet (4-bead sc): Insert hook in indicated st, yo, draw up a lp, move 4 beads up next to work, yo, draw through 2 lps on hook.

5-bead single crochet (5-bead sc): Insert hook in indicated st, yo, draw up a lp, move 5 beads up next

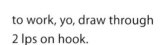

to work, yo, draw through 2 lps on hook.

SHAWL

Row 1: With 1 strand each cream and gold, ch 12, **extended dc** *(see Special Stitches)* in 4th ch from hook, extended dc in each rem ch across, turn.
(3 blocks)

Rows 2–105: Follow Chart *(see Fig. 1)*, working blocks and mesh as indicated, using Special Stitches as a guide, turn at end of each row.

Top edging

Row 106: Ch 1, sc in first extended dc, [ch 1, sk 1 extended dc, sc in next extended dc] across, turn.

Row 107: Sl st into ch-1 sp, ch 1, (sc, ch 2, sc) in same ch-1 sp as beg ch-1, [(sc, ch 2, sc) in next ch-1 sp] across, fasten off.

Beaded Edging

Note: String 2,875 beads onto cream crochet cotton. This is approximately 35 extra beads.

With WS facing, attach cream to upper corner of Shawl and, working in side edge of rows, ch 1, **bead sc** *(see Special Stitches)* in same st as beg ch-1, Beaded Edging is worked in this manner, **3-bead sc** *(see Special Stitches)* in the side post of each extended dc going down *(vertical)*, 3-bead sc in each st of each block exposed on row *(horizontal)*. Continue across the Shawl in this manner to the center 3 blocks at the beg of the Shawl *(row 1)*, work across these 10 sts, 3-bead sc twice, **4-bead sc**

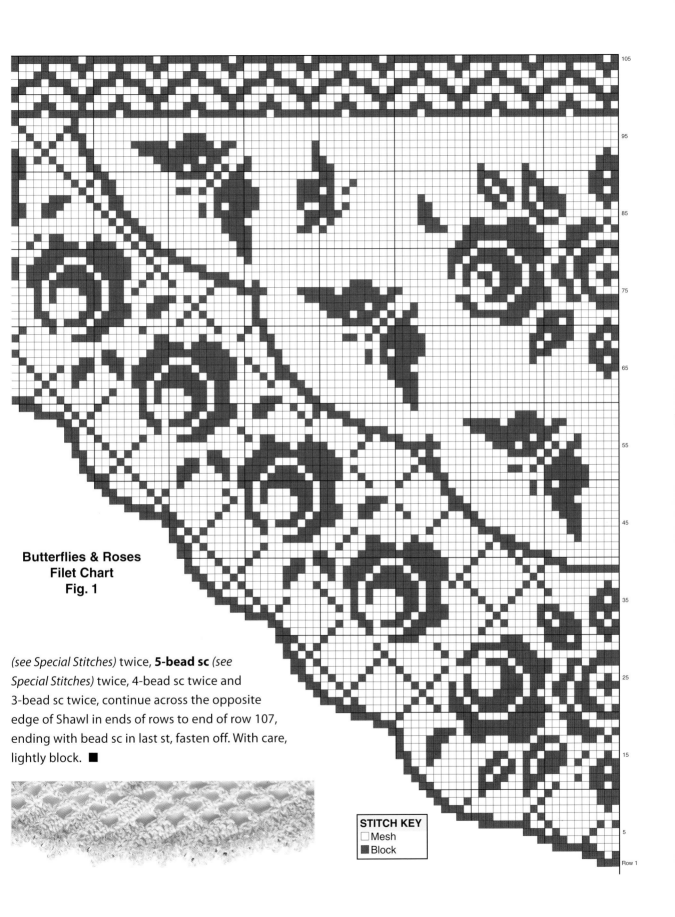

**Butterflies & Roses
Filet Chart
Fig. 1**

(see Special Stitches) twice, **5-bead sc** *(see Special Stitches)* twice, 4-bead sc twice and 3-bead sc twice, continue across the opposite edge of Shawl in ends of rows to end of row 107, ending with bead sc in last st, fasten off. With care, lightly block. ■

STITCH KEY
☐ Mesh
■ Block

105
95
85
75
65
55
45
35
25
15
5
Row 1

SUNSET PONCHO

DESIGN BY MARY JANE PROTUS FOR COATS & CLARK

EASY

Finished Size

One size fits most women

Finished Garment Measurement

21 inches long x 60-inch circumference

Materials

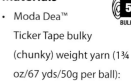

- Moda Dea™ Ticker Tape bulky (chunky) weight yarn (1¾ oz/67 yds/50g per ball):
  10 balls #9273 sunset
- Size N/15/10mm crochet hook or size needed to obtain gauge
- Tapestry needle
- Stitch markers

Gauge

[Sk next 3 tr, 4 tr in next sc, ch 4, sc in next tr] = 3½ inches; 4 rows = 3¼ inches

Pattern Notes

Weave in loose ends as work progresses.
Join rounds with a slip stitch unless otherwise stated.

PONCHO

Body

Row 1 (WS): Ch 54, sc in 2nd ch from hook, [sk next 3 chs, 4 tr in next ch, ch 4, sk next 3 chs, sc in next ch] 6 times, sk next 3 chs, 4 tr in last ch, turn.

Row 2: Ch 1, sc in first tr, [sk next 3 tr, 4 tr in next sc, ch 4, sc in next tr] 6 times, sk next 3 tr, 4 tr in last sc, turn.

Rep row 2 until Body measures 60 inches, ending on WS.

Last row: Ch 1, sc in first tr, [ch 3, sk next 3 tr, sc in next sc, ch 3, sc in next tr] 6 times, ch 3, sk next 3 tr, sc in last sc, fasten off.

Place st marker on right edge at 16 inches *(side seam)*, then measure 28 inches and place another st marker *(neck opening)*, then measure 16 inches and place the last st marker *(side seam)*. Fold fabric in half, and, working through both thicknesses, sew seam from beg to first st marker, remove marker, fasten off, sk 28 inches, sew seam from st marker to end.

Neckline Trim

Rnd 1 (RS): Attach yarn at seam, ch 1, sc evenly spaced around neckline opening, join in beg sc, fasten off.

Edging

Rnd 1 (RS): Attach yarn at seam, ch 1, sc evenly spaced across to corner, (sc, ch 1, sc) in corner, ch 4, *sk tr row end, sc in sc row end, ch 4, rep from * to next corner, (sc, ch 1, sc) in corner, sc evenly spaced across to first sc, join in beg sc, fasten off.

Fringe

Cut 22-inch lengths of sunset, holding 2 strands tog, fold in half forming a lp, insert hook into any sc along long edge, or into the ch-1 sp at corner, working from WS of the body and into the lp, draw the lp through, draw yarn ends through lp on hook, pull gently to secure. Trim ends. ■

COZY CAFÉ AU LAIT SHRUG

DESIGN BY JEWDY LAMBERT

EASY

Finished Size

Shrug measures 18 x 60 inches, excluding Cuffs. Each Cuff measures 2 inches.

Materials

- King Cole Luxury Mohair bulky (chunky) weight yarn (1¾ oz/110 yds/50g per ball): 4 balls #261 Vienna
- Size K/10½/6.5mm crochet hook or size needed to obtain gauge
- Tapestry needle

5 BULKY

Gauge

8 dc = 3 inches; 6 dc rows = 4 inches

Pattern Notes

Weave in loose ends as work progresses.

Join rounds with a slip stitch unless otherwise stated.

For individual sizing, measure from wrist of outstretched arm across shoulders behind nape of neck to wrist of opposite outstretched arm. Make a chain the length of this measured distance; if working pattern for larger sizes, add several rows as desired to the Body. Work Sleeve Shaping and Cuffs as indicated working 1 additional st into each row on each Cuff.

SHRUG

Body

Row 1: Ch 149, dc in 4th ch from hook, dc in each rem ch across, turn. *(146 dc)*

Row 2: Ch 3 *(counts as first dc)*, dc in each dc across, turn.

Rows 3–25: Rep row 2. At the end of row 25, do not fasten off.

CONTINUED ON PAGE 80

RUFFLED SHOULDER WRAP

DESIGN BY JOYCE BRAGG

INTERMEDIATE

Finished Sizes

Instructions given fit 28–30-inch bust (X-small); changes for 32–34-inch bust (small), 36–38-inch bust (medium), 40–42-inch bust (large), 44–46-inch bust (X-large), 48–50-inch bust (2X-large) and 52–54-inch bust (3X-large) are in [ ].

Gauge

3 dc = 1 inch; 2 dc rnds = 1 inch

Pattern Notes

Weave in loose ends as work progresses.

Join rounds with a slip stitch unless otherwise stated.

WRAP

Body

Rnd 1: Starting at center back, ch 10, join in first ch to form a ring, ch 2 (counts as first hdc), 19 hdc in ring, join in 2nd ch of beg ch-2. (20 hdc)

Rnd 2: Ch 2, 2 hdc in next hdc, [hdc in next hdc, 2 hdc in next hdc] around, join in 2nd ch of beg ch-2. (30 hdc)

Rnd 3: Ch 2, hdc in each of next 5 hdc, ch 3, [hdc in

Materials

- Patons Glittallic bulky (chunky) weight yarn (1¾ oz/61 yds/50g per skein):
  7 [7, 8, 9, 9, 10, 10] skeins #66008 cream gleam
- Size K/10½/6.5mm crochet hook or size needed to obtain gauge
- Tapestry needle
- 1½-inch shank button

5 BULKY

each of next 6 hdc, ch 3] 4 times, join in 2nd ch of beg ch-2. (30 hdc, 5 ch-3 sps)

Rnd 4: Ch 2, hdc in each of next 5 hdc, ch 3, dc in next ch-3 sp, ch 3, [hdc in each of next 6 hdc, ch 3, dc in next ch-3 sp, ch 3] around, join in 2nd ch of beg ch-2. (30 hdc, 10 ch-3 sps, 5 dc)

Rnd 5: Ch 2, hdc in each of next 5 hdc, *ch 3, dc in next ch-3 sp, ch 3, dc in next ch-3 sp, ch 3**, hdc in each of next 6 hdc, rep from * around, ending last rep at **, join in 2nd ch of beg ch-2. (30 hdc, 15 ch-3 sps, 10 dc)

Rnd 6: Ch 3 (counts as first dc), dc in each hdc, 3 dc in each ch-3 sp, dc in each dc around, join in 3rd ch of beg ch-3. (85 dc)

For Sizes Medium, Large, X-Large, 2X-Large & 3X-Large Only

Rnd 7: Ch 3, dc in each st around, join in 3rd ch of beg ch-3.

For All Sizes

Rnd 7 [7, 8, 8, 8, 8, 8]: Ch 6 (counts as first dc, ch-3), sk next dc, dc in next dc, [ch 3, sk next dc, dc in next dc] around, join in 3rd ch of beg ch-6. (43 dc, 43 ch-3 sps)

Rnd 8 [8, 9, 9, 9, 9, 9]: Ch 6, [dc in center ch of ch-3 sp, ch 3] around, join in 3rd ch of beg ch-3. (43 dc)

For Sizes Small, Medium, Large, X-Large, 2X-Large & 3X-Large Only

Rnd 9 [10, 10, 10, 10, 10]: Rep rnd 8 [9, 9, 9, 9, 9].

For Sizes Medium, Large, X-Large, 2X-Large & 3X-Large Only
Rnd 11 [12, 13, 14, 14]: [Rep rnd 9 [9, 9, 9, 9] 1 [2, 3, 4, 4] times.

For All Sizes
Rnd 9 [10, 12, 13, 14, 15, 15]: Sl st in center ch of ch-3 sp, ch 3, dc in same ch, ch 3, [2 dc in center ch of next ch-3 sp, ch 3] around, join in 3rd ch of beg ch-3. *(86 dc, 43 ch-3 sps)*
Rnd 10 [11, 13, 14, 15, 16, 16]: Rep rnd 9 [10, 12, 13, 14, 15, 15].
Rnd 11 [12, 14, 15, 16, 17, 17]: Sl st in center ch of ch-3 sp, ch 3, dc in same ch, [ch 3, 2 dc in center ch of next ch-3 sp] around, ending with 2 dc in center ch of last ch-3 sp, do not ch-3, join in 3rd ch of beg ch-3. *(86 dc, 42 ch-3 sps)*
Rnd 12 [13, 15, 16, 17, 18, 18]: Sl st in center ch of ch-3 sp, ch 5 *(counts as first dc, ch-2)*, 4 dc in each of next 7 ch-3 sps, [ch 2, 4 dc in each of next 7 ch-3 sps] 4 times, ch 2, 4 dc in each of next 6 ch-3 sps, 3 dc in same ch sp as beg ch-5, join in 3rd ch of beg ch-5. *(168 dc, 6 ch-2 sps)*
Rnd 13 [14, 16, 17, 18, 19, 19]: Sl st into ch-2 sp, ch 4 *(counts as first hdc, ch-2)*, hdc in each of next 28 dc, [ch 2, hdc in next ch-2 sp, ch 2, hdc in each of next 28 dc] around, ending with ch 2, join in 2nd ch of beg ch-4.
Rnd 14 [15, 17, 18, 19, 20, 20]: Sl st into ch-2 sp, ch 4, *hdc in each of next 28 hdc**, [ch 2, hdc in next ch-2 sp] twice, ch 2, rep from * around, ending last rep at **, ch 2, hdc in next ch-2 sp, ch 2, join in 2nd ch of beg ch-4.
Rnd 15 [16, 18, 19, 20, 21, 21]: Sl st into ch-2 sp, ch 4, *hdc in each of next 28 hdc**, [ch 2, hdc in next ch-2 sp] 3 times, ch 2, rep from * around, ending last rep at **, [ch 2, hdc in next ch-2 sp] twice, ch 2, join in 2nd ch of beg ch-4.
Rnd 16 [17, 19, 20, 21, 22, 22]: Ch 3, [3 dc in each ch-2 sp, dc in each hdc] around, join in 3rd ch of beg ch-3.
Rnd 17 [18, 20, 21, 22, 23, 23]: Ch 6, sk next dc, [dc in next dc, ch 3, sk next dc] around, join in 3rd ch of beg ch-6.
Rnd 18 [19, 21, 22, 23, 24, 24]: Sl st in center ch of ch-3 sp, ch 6, [dc in center ch of next ch-3 sp, ch 3] around, join in 3rd ch of beg ch-6.

CONTINUED ON PAGE 80

TRIANGLES SHAWL

DESIGN BY NAZANIN FARD

EASY

Finished Size

48 inches across top x
44 inches each side,
excluding Tassels

Materials

- Aunt Lydia's Fashion Crochet
  size 3 crochet cotton (150
  yds per ball):
  5 balls each #325
  tangerine *(A)* and
  #625 sage *(B)*
- Size E/4/3.5mm crochet
  hook or size needed to
  obtain gauge
- Tapestry needle

Gauge

6 sc = 1 inch

Pattern Notes

Weave in loose ends as work progresses.
Join rounds with a slip stitch unless otherwise stated.
Shawl switches between A and B for each triangle.
There is a total of 81 motifs, 36 motifs with rnds 1–4
crocheted with B and rnds 5 and 6 crocheted with A
and 45 motifs with rnds 1–4 crocheted with A and rnds
5 and 6 crocheted with B.

SHAWL

First Motif

Rnd 1: With A, ch 6, join in first ch to form a ring, ch 1,
12 sc in ring, join in beg sc. *(12 sc)*

Rnd 2: Ch 10 *(counts as first dc, ch-7)*, *sk next sc, dc in
next sc, ch 3**, sk next sc, dc in next sc, ch 7, rep from *
around, ending last rep at ** , join in 3rd ch of beg ch-
10. *(3 ch-7 sps, 3 ch-3 sps)*

Rnd 3: Ch 3 (counts as first dc), 3 dc in next ch sp, *ch 6, 4 dc in same ch sp, 3 dc in next ch sp**, 4 dc in next ch sp, rep from * around, ending last rep at **, join in 3rd ch of beg ch-3.

Rnd 4: Sl st in next dc, ch 6 (counts as first dc, ch-3), *(4 dc, ch 5, 4 dc) in next ch sp, ch 3, sk next 2 dc, dc in next dc, ch 3, sk next 2 dc, sc in next dc, ch 3**, sk next 2 dc, dc in next dc, ch 3, rep from * around, ending last rep at **, join in 3rd ch of beg ch-3, fasten off.

Rnd 5: Join B to any unused sc of rnd 1, ch 1, sc in same sc as beg ch-1, ch 3, [sc in next sc of rnd 1, ch 3] around, join in beg sc. (6 ch-3 sps)

Rnd 6: Ch 1, (sc, hdc, 3 dc, hdc, sc) in each ch-3 sp around, join in beg sc, fasten off.

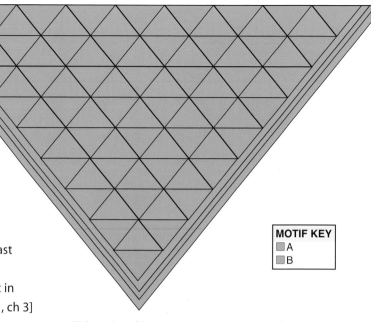

MOTIF KEY
- A
- B

**Triangles Shawl Motif
Assembly Diagram
Fig. 1**

2nd Motif

Rnds 1–3: With B, rep rnds 1–3 of First Motif.

Rnd 4: Sl st into next dc, ch 6, *4 dc in next ch sp, ch 2, sl st in corresponding ch-5 sp of previous motif, ch 2, 4 dc in same ch sp, ch 1, sl st in corresponding ch-3 sp of previous motif, ch 1, sk next 2 dc, dc in next dc, ch 3, sk next 2 dc, sc in next dc, ch 3, sk next 2 dc, dc in next dc, ch 1, sl st in corresponding ch-3 sp of previous motif, ch 1, rep from * to join to adjacent motifs, otherwise work the same as rnd 4 for First Motif, fasten off.

Rnds 5 & 6: Join A, rep rnds 5 and 6 of First Motif.

Rem Motifs

Rep as for 2nd Motif alternating A and B as indicated in Motif Assembly Diagram (Fig. 1).

Border

Row 1: Join B to left side of top corner of Shawl, ch 7, sc in same ch sp, *[ch 7, sc in next ch sp] 4 times, ch 7, sc in the joining of the chs of next 2 Motifs, rep from * to point of Shawl, ch 7, sc in same ch sp, rep from * to next corner, ending with ch 7, sc in same ch sp, turn.

Row 2: [Ch 7, sc in next ch sp] across to bottom point, ch 7, sc in same ch sp, [ch 7, sc in next ch sp] across to next point, fasten off.

Row 3: Join A in first ch sp of previous row, ch 7, sc in same ch sp, [ch 7, sc in next ch sp] across to bottom point, ch 7, sc in same ch sp, [ch 7, sc in next ch sp] across to next point, turn.

Row 4: Rep row 2.

Row 5: Join B, rep row 3.

Row 6: Rep row 2.

Fringe

Cut 2-12-inch strands of both A and B. Hold strands tog, fold in half, insert hook in ch sp of row 6, draw strands through at fold to form a lp on hook, draw cut ends through lp on hook, pull gently to secure. ■

PEEKABOO PONCHO

DESIGN BY JEWDY LAMBERT

EASY

Finished Sizes

Instructions given fit 32–36-inch bust *(small/medium)*; changes for 38–42-inch bust *(medium/large)* and 44–50-inch bust *(X-large/2X-large)* are in [ ].

Materials

- Moda Dea™ Beadnik medium (worsted) weight yarn (1¾ oz/103 yds/50g per ball): 5 [6, 6] balls #2914 blue beat
- Size I/9/5.5mm crochet hook or size needed to obtain gauge
- Tapestry needle

Gauge

6 tr = 2 inches; 2 tr rnds = 1¾ inches

Pattern Notes

Weave in loose ends as work progresses.

Join rounds with a slip stitch unless otherwise stated.

Additional yarn is required for longer Ponchos.

PONCHO

Body

Foundation rnd (RS): Beg at neckline, ch 100 [108, 116], taking care not to twist, join in first ch to form a ring, ch 3 *(counts as first dc)*, dc in each of next 23 [25, 27] chs, (dc, ch 5, dc) in next ch, [dc in each of next 24 {26, 28} chs, (dc, ch 5, dc) in next ch] around, join in 3rd ch of beg ch-3, turn.

Rnd 1: Ch 4 *(counts as first tr)*, tr in each dc around and 7 tr in each ch-5 sp, join in 4th ch of beg ch-4, turn.

Rnd 2: Ch 4, tr in each tr around, work (tr, ch 5, tr) in 4th tr of each 7-tr group, join in 4th ch of beg ch-4, turn.

Rnd 3: Ch 4, tr in each tr around, working 7 tr in each ch-5 sp around, join in 4th ch of beg ch-4, turn.

Rnds 4–13: [Rep rnds 2 and 3 alternately] 5 times. At the end of rnd 13, fasten off or for longer Poncho continue to rep rnds 2 and 3 alternately to desired length. ■

COOL CLASS DRESS & SHOULDER COVER

DESIGNS BY SVETLANA AVRAKH

INTERMEDIATE

Finished Sizes

Dress: Instructions given fit 28–
34-inch bust *(X-small/small)*;
changes for 36–38-inch bust
(medium), 40–42-inch bust
(large) and 44–46-inch bust
(X-large) are in [ ].

Shoulder Cover: Instructions
given fit X-small/small;
changes for medium and
large/X-large are in [ ].

Finished Garment Measurements

Dress Bust: 37 inches *(X-small/
small)* [41 inches *(medium)*,
45 inches *(large)*, 49½ inches
(X-large)]

Shoulder Cover Cuff to Cuff:
18 inches *(X-small/small)* [19
inches *(medium)*, 20 inches
(large/X-large)]

Width of Back: 16 inches
(X-small/small) [16 inches
(medium), 17 inches
(large/X-large)]

Materials

- Patons Brilliant
  light (light
  worsted) weight
  yarn (1¾ oz/166
  yds/50g per skein):
  9 [10, 11, 12] skeins
  #03023 gold glow
- Patons Silverlash medium
  (worsted) weight yarn (1¾
  oz/164 yds/50g per skein):
  2 skeins #81008
  crystallite cream
- Sizes F/5/3.75mm and
  N/15/10mm crochet
  hooks or sizes needed to
  obtain gauge
- Tapestry needle
- Stitch markers
- Straight pins

Gauge

Size F hook: 9 sc = 2 inches; 21 rows = 4 inches
Size N hook: 6 sts = 2 inches; 2 rows = 2 inches

Pattern Notes

Weave in loose ends as work progresses.
Join rounds with a slip stitch unless otherwise stated.

Special Stitches

V-stitch (V-st): (Hdc, ch 1, hdc) in indicated st.
Beginning V-stitch (beg V-st): Ch 3 *(counts as first hdc, ch-1)*, hdc in same st as beg ch-3.
Beginning decrease (beg dec): Ch 2 *(counts as first dc)*, yo, insert hook in next sc, yo, draw up a lp, [yo, draw through 2 lps on hook] twice.
Ending decrease (ending dec): Yo, insert hook in indicated st, yo, draw up a lp, yo, draw through 2 lps on hook, yo, insert hook in next st, yo, draw up a lp, yo, draw through 2 lps on hook, yo, draw through all lps on hook.

DRESS

Back

Row 1 (RS): With size F hook and gold glow, ch 100 [109, 118, 130], hdc in 4th ch from hook *(counts as first V-st)*, *ch 1, sk next 2 chs, **V-st** (see Special Stitches) in next ch, rep from * across, turn. *(33 [36, 39, 43] V-sts)*
Row 2: Sl st in ch-1 sp of first V-st, ch 4 *(counts as first dc, ch-1)*, *sc in next ch-1 sp, ch 1, dc in next V-st, ch 1, rep from * across, ending with dc in last V-st, turn.

Row 3: Beg V-st (*see Special Stitches*) in first dc, *ch 1, sk next sc, V-st in next dc, rep from * across, ending with V-st in 3rd ch of beg ch-4, turn.

Rep rows 2 and 3 until piece measures 14 inches.

Row 4 (RS): Beg dec (*see Special Stitches*), ch 1, V-st in next dc, *ch 1, sk next sc, V-st in next dc, rep from * to last sc and dc, **ending dec** (*see Special Stitches*) in last sc and dc, turn. (*31 [34, 37, 41] V-sts*)

Row 5 (WS): Ch 1, sc in first st, *ch 1, dc in next V-st, ch 1, sc in next ch-1 sp, rep from * across, ending with dc in last V-st, sc in last st, turn.

Row 6 (RS): Ch 4, *V-st in next dc, sk next sc, ch 1, rep from * across, ending with dc in last sc, turn.

Rep rows 5 and 6 until piece measures 21 inches, ending with a RS row, turn.

Row 7 (WS): Beg dec in first V-st and dc, *ch 1, sc in next ch-1 sp, ch 1, dc in next V-st, rep from * to last V-st, ch 1, ending dec in V-st and dc, turn.

Row 8: Beg V-st, *ch 1, sk next sc, V-st in next dc, rep from * across, ending with V-st in last st, turn. (*31 [34, 37, 41] V-sts*)

Row 9: Sl st in ch-1 sp of first V-st, ch 4, *sc in next ch-1 sp, ch 1, dc in next V-st, ch 1, rep from * across, ending with dc in last V-st, turn.

Rep rows 8 and 9 alternately until piece measures 28 inches, ending with a RS row, turn.

Armhole Shaping

Row 1: Sl st in each st to 3rd V-st, ch 4, *sc in next ch-1 sp, ch 1, dc in next V-st, ch 1, rep from * to last 3 V-sts, dc in next V-st, leaving rem 2 V-sts unworked, turn.

Row 2: Beg dec in first st and next sc, V-st in next dc, *ch 1, sk next sc, V-st in next dc, rep from * to last sc and dc, ending dec in sc and dc, turn. (*25 [28, 31, 35] V-sts*)

Row 3: Beg dec in first st and next V-st, *ch 1, sc in next ch-1 sp, ch 1, dc in next V-st, ch 1, rep from * to last V-st, ending dec in V-st and last st, turn.

[Rep rows 2 and 3 of Armhole Shaping alternately] 1 [2, 3, 4] times. (*23 [24, 25, 27] V-sts*)

Row 4: Beg V-st, *ch 1, sk next sc, V-st in next dc, rep from * across, ending with V-st in last st, turn.

Row 5: Sl st in ch-1 sp of first V-st, ch 4, *sc in next ch-1 sp, ch 1, dc in next V-st, ch 1, rep from * across, ending with dc in last V-st, turn.

Rep rows 4 and 5 alternately until Armhole measures 7 [7, 8, 8] inches, ending with a RS row, turn.

First Neck Shaping

Row 1: Sl st in ch-1 sp of first V-st, ch 4, [sc in next ch-1 sp, ch 1, dc in next V-st, ch 1] 4 [4, 5, 5] times, omitting ch-1 at end of last rep, ending dec in next ch-1 sp and V-st, leaving rem sts unworked, turn.

Row 2: Sl st in next dc, beg V-st, *ch 1, sk next sc, V-st in next dc, rep from * across, fasten off.

2nd Neck Shaping

Row 1: With WS facing, sk next 11 [12, 11, 13] V-sts, attach gold glow with sl st in next V-st, beg dec, *ch 1, sc in next ch-1 sp, ch 1, dc in next V-st, rep from * across, turn.

Row 2: Beg V-st, *ch 1, sk next sc, V-st in next dc, rep from * to last 2 sts, V-st in next dc, fasten off.

Front

Rep Back to Armhole Shaping.

Armhole Shaping

Row 1: Rep row 1 of Armhole Shaping.

Rep rows 2 and 3 of Armhole Shaping alternately until Armhole measures 3 [3, 4, 4] inches.

First Neck Shaping

Row 1: Sl st in ch-1 sp of first V-st, ch 4, [sc in next ch-1 sp, ch 1, dc in next V-st, ch 1] 7 [7, 8, 8] times, omitting ch-1 at end of last rep, ending dec in next ch-1 sp and V-st, leaving rem sts unworked, turn.

Row 2: Sl st in next dc, beg V-st, *ch 1, sk next sc, V-st in next dc, rep from * across, ending with V-st in 3rd ch of ch-4.

Row 3: Sl st in ch-1 sp of first V-st, ch 4, *sc in next ch-1 sp, ch 1, dc in next V-st, ch 1, rep from * to last V-st, omitting last ch-1 at end of last rep, ending dec in next ch-1 sp and V-st, turn.

[Rep rows 2 and 3] 3 times for each size. (5 [5, 6, 6] V-sts) Work even until Front Neck Shaping is same length as Back Neck Shaping, fasten off.

2nd Neck Shaping

Row 1: With WS facing, sk next 7 [8, 7, 9] V-sts, attach gold glow with sl st in next V-st, beg dec in next 2 sts, *ch 1, sc in next ch-1 sp, ch 1, dc in next V-st, rep from * across, turn.

Row 2: Beg V-st, *ch 1, sk next sc, V-st in next dc, rep from * to last 2 sts, V-st in next dc, turn.

Row 3: Beg dec in first V-st and next ch-1 sp, *dc in next V-st, ch 1, sc in next ch-1 sp, ch 1, rep from * to end of row, ending with 1 dc in last V-st, turn.

Work even until Front Neck Shaping is same length as Back Neck Shaping, fasten off.

Finishing

Pin garment pieces to measurements. Cover with a damp cloth, leave cloth to dry. Sew side and shoulder seams.

Neckline Trim

Rnd 1 (RS): Attach gold glow with sl st at left shoulder seam, ch 1, sc evenly spaced around neckline opening, join in beg sc.

Rnds 2–4: Ch 1, sc in each sc around, join in beg sc.

Rnd 5: Ch 1, **reverse sc** *(see Fig. 1)* in each st around, join in beg sc, fasten off.

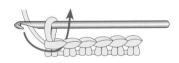

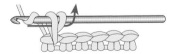

Reverse Single Crochet
Fig. 1

Armhole Trim

Rnd 1 (RS): Attach gold glow with sl st in side seam, ch 1, sc evenly sp around Armhole opening, join in beg sc.

Rnds 2–4: Ch 1, **sc dec** *(see Stitch Guide)* in next 2 sc, sc in each sc to last 2 sc, sc dec in next 2 sc, join in beg sc.

CONTINUED ON PAGE 81

LILAC SHAWL

DESIGN BY JOSIE RABIER

INTERMEDIATE

Finished Size

60 inches across x 32 inches deep, excluding Fringe

Materials

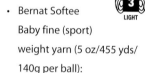

- Bernat Softee Baby fine (sport) weight yarn (5 oz/455 yds/140g per ball):
  3 balls #30185 soft lilac
- G/6/4mm crochet hook or size needed to obtain gauge

Gauge

4 dc = 1 inch, 2 dc rows = 1 inch

Special Stitches

Joining: Ch 2, sl st in 3rd ch of corresponding or next ch-5 sp of other Motif, ch 2.

Split popcorn (split pc): 4 dc in each of next 2 ch sps, drop lp from hook, insert hook in first st of 8 dc group, pull dropped lp through, ch 1.

Picot: Ch 9, sl st in 9th ch from hook.

SHAWL

First Row

First Motif

Rnd 1: Ch 4, sl st in first ch to form ring, ch 3 *(counts as first dc)*, 19 dc in ring, join with sl st in 3rd ch of beg ch-3. *(20 dc)*

Rnd 2: Ch 3 *(counts as first dc)*, dc in same st, 2 dc in each st around, join with sl st in 3rd ch of beg ch-3. *(40 dc)*

Rnd 3: Ch 3, dc in each of next 4 sts, ch 7, [dc in each of next 5 sts, ch 7] around, join with sl st in 3rd ch of beg ch-3. *(40 dc, 8 ch sps)*

Rnd 4: Ch 3, dc in each of next 4 sts, *ch 3, sl st in center ch of next ch-7, ch 3**, dc in each of next 5 sts, rep from * around, ending last rep at **, join with sl st in 3rd ch of beg ch-3. *(40 dc, 16 ch sps)*

Rnd 5: Ch 2 *(ch-2 is not used or counted as st)*, **dc dec** *(see Stitch Guide)* in next 4 sts, *ch 5, sl st in next sl st between ch-3 sps, ch 5**, dc dec in next 5 sts, rep from * around, ending last rep at **, join with sl st in top of beg dc. *(8 dc, 16 ch sps)*

Rnd 6: Ch 8 *(counts as first dc, ch-5)*, dc in same st, *sl st in next ch sp, ({dc, ch 5} twice, dc) in next sl st *(corner)*, sl st in next ch sp, (dc, ch 5, dc) in next dc, sl st in next ch sp, (dc, ch 5, dc) in next sl st, sl st in next ch sp**, (dc, ch 5, dc) in next dc, rep from * around ending last rep at **, join with sl st in 3rd ch of beg ch-8. Fasten off.

2nd Motif

Rnds 1–5: Rep rnds 1–5 of First Motif.

Rnd 6: Ch 8, dc in same st, sl st in next ch sp, (dc, ch 5, dc) in next sl st, joining to side of last Motif, work **joining** *(see Special Stitches)*, dc in same sl st in this Motif, sl st in next ch sp, dc in next dc, work joining, dc in same dc on this Motif, sl st in next ch sp, dc in next sl st, work joining, dc in same sl st on this Motif, sl st in next ch sp, dc in next dc, work joining, dc in same dc on this Motif, sl st in next ch sp, dc in next sl st, work joining, dc in same sl st on this Motif, (ch 5, dc) in same sl st, *sl st in next ch sp, (dc, ch 5, dc) in next dc, sl st in next ch sp, (dc, ch 5, dc) in next sl st, sl st in next ch sp**, (dc, ch 5, dc) in next dc, sl st in next ch sp, ({dc, ch 5} twice, dc) in next sl st, rep from * around ending last rep at **, join with sl st in 3rd ch of beg ch-8. Fasten off.

Rep 2nd Motif 5 times for total of 7 Motifs on this row.

2nd Row

First Motif

Joining to bottom of 2nd Motif on last row, work same as First Row 2nd Motif.

2nd Motif

Rnds 1–5: Rep rnds 1–5 of First Row First Motif.

Rnd 6: Ch 8, dc in same st, sl st in next ch sp, (dc, ch 5, dc) in next sl st, joining to bottom of next Motif on last row, work joining, dc in same sl st in this Motif, *sl st in next ch sp, dc in next dc, work joining, dc in same dc on this Motif, sl st in next ch sp, dc in next sl st, work joining, dc in same sl st on this Motif, sl st in next ch sp, dc in next dc, work joining, dc in same dc on this Motif, sl st in next ch sp, dc in next sl st, work joining, dc in same sl st on this Motif*, joining to side of last Motif on this row, work joining, dc in same sl st on this Motif, rep between *, (ch 5, dc) in same sl st, sl st in next ch sp, (dc, ch 5, dc) in next dc, sl st in next ch sp, (dc, ch 5, dc) in next sl st, sl st in next ch sp, (dc, ch 5, dc) in next dc, sl st in next ch sp, ({dc, ch 5} twice, dc) in next sl st, sl st in next ch sp, (dc, ch 5, dc) in next dc, sl st in next ch sp, (dc, ch 5, dc) in next sl st, sl st in next ch sp, join with sl st in 3rd ch of beg ch-8. Fasten off.
Rep 2nd Motif 3 times for total of 5 Motifs.

3rd Row

First Motif

Joining to bottom of 2nd Motif on last row, work same as First Row 2nd Motif.

2nd Motif

Work same as 2nd Row 2nd Motif.
Rep 2nd Motif once for total of 3 Motifs on this row.

4th Row

First Motif

Joining to bottom of 2nd Motif on last row, work same as First Row 2nd Motif.

Border Motif

Row 1: Ch 4, sl st in first ch to form ring, ch 4 *(counts as first tr)*, 10 dc in ring, tr in ring, turn. *(10 dc, 2 tr)*

Row 2: Ch 4, 2 dc in each dc across, tr in last tr, turn. *(20 dc, 2 tr)*

Row 3: Ch 4, dc in each of next 10 sts, ch 5, dc in each of next 10 sts, tr in last st, turn.

Row 4: Ch 4, dc in each of next 10 sts, ch 5, sl st in next ch sp, ch 5, dc in each of next 10 sts, tr in last st, turn.

Row 5: Ch 4, dc in each of next 4 sts, sk next 2 sts, dc in each of next 4 sts, [ch 5, sl st in next ch sp] twice, ch 5, dc in each of next 4 sts, sk next 2 sts, dc in each of next 4 sts, tr in last st, turn.

Row 6: Ch 4, dc in each of next 3 sts, sk next 2 sts, dc in each of next 3 sts, [ch 5, sl st in next ch sp] 3 times, ch 5, dc in each of next 3 sts, sk next 2 sts, dc in each of next 3 sts, tr in last st, turn.

Row 7: Ch 4, dc in each of next 2 sts, sk next 2 sts, dc in each of next 2 sts, [ch 5, sl st in next ch sp] 4 times, ch 5, dc in each of next 2 sts, sk next 2 sts, dc in each of next 2 sts, tr in last st, turn.

Row 8: Ch 4, dc in next dc, sk next 2 sts, dc in next st, [ch 5, sl st in next ch sp] 5 times, ch 5, dc in next dc, sk next 2 sts, dc in next st, tr in last st, turn.

Rnd 9: Now working in rnds, ch 9 *(counts as first tr, ch-5)*, sk next 2 dc, sl st in next ch sp, [ch 5, sl st in next ch sp] 5 times, ch 5, tr in last st, working in ends of rows, dc in end of next row, ch 2, working on last Motifs at end of first 2 rows, sl st in center ch of 5th ch sp from joining on First Motif, ch 2, dc in same row on this Motif, *sl st in next row, dc in end of next row, ch 2, sl st in center ch of next ch sp on other Motif, ch 2, dc in same row on this Motif*, rep between * twice, dc in next beg ring, ch 2, dc in center ch of next ch sp on other Motif, dc in same ring on this Motif, ch 2, working on next Motif at end of row, sl st in center ch sp of next ch sp after joining on other Motif, ch 2, dc in same ring on this Motif, rep between * 4 times, join with sl st in 3rd ch of beg ch-9.

Rep in each indentation between rows on each side of Shawl, ending with 3 Border Motifs on each side.

Filler Motif

Working in sps between joined Motifs *(there are 8 ch-2 sps at center)*, join in any ch sp, ch 3, 3 dc in same sp, 4 dc in next ch sp, drop lp from hook, insert hook in top of ch-3, pull dropped lp through, [**split pc** *(see Special Stitches)*] 3 times, join with sl st in sp between first and 2nd pc. Fasten off.

Work a Filler Motif in each sp between Motifs.

Edging

Note: In the following rnd, sl st in dc between ch-5 sps.
With RS facing, join with sl st in center corner dc of top right-hand corner Motif before long straight edge, work the Edging in the following steps:

A. *(3 hdc, **picot**—*see Special Stitches*, 3 hdc) in each of next 5 ch-5 sps, 2 hdc in next ch-2 sp, picot, 2 hdc in next ch-2 sp, rep from * 5 times, (3 hdc, picot, 3 hdc) in each of next 10 ch-5 sps, 2 hdc in next ch-2 sp, picot, 2 hdc in next ch-2 sp;

B. *(3 hdc, picot, 3 hdc) in each of next 7 ch-5 sps, 2 hdc in next ch-2 sp, picot, 2 hdc in each of next 2 ch-2 sps, picot, 2 hdc in next ch-2 sp, rep from *, (3 hdc, picot, 3 hdc) in each of next 7 ch-5 sps;

C. 2 hdc in next ch-2 sp, picot, 2 hdc in next ch-2 sp, (3 hdc, picot, 3 hdc) in each of next 5 ch-5 sps, 2 hdc in next ch-2 sp, picot, 2 hdc in next ch-2 sp;

D. Rep step B;

E. 2 hdc in next ch-2 sp, picot, 2 hdc in next ch-2 sp, (3 hdc, picot, 3 hdc) in each of last 5 ch-5 sps, join with sl st in beg sl st. Fasten off.

Fringe

For each Fringe, cut 7 strands each 13 inches in length. With all strands held tog, fold in half, insert hook in each picot st of E, pull fold through, pull all loose ends through fold, tighten. Trim.

Attach Fringe in each picot on sides and bottom edge of Shawl. ■

GOLD NUGGET COCKTAIL COVER-UP CONTINUED FROM PAGE 53

With RS tog, sew 3 Squares tog according to diagram *(see Fig. 1)*. Sew Shoulder Pieces as indicated on diagram.

Trim

Working around bottom edge, join 24K with sl st in any tr, ch 4 *(counts as first tr)*, tr in each tr and in each ch sp around with 2 tr in each joining, join with sl st in top of ch-4. Fasten off.

Rep around neck edge, working **tr dec** *(see Stitch Guide)* in 3 sts at each V.

Drawstring

With 24K, leaving 5-inch length at beg and end, make ch 55 inches in length. Fasten off.
Weave drawstring through sts around neck edge beg and ending in front.

Fringe

Cut one strand Eros, 18 inches long, fold strand in half, insert hook in st, draw fold through st on hook to form a lp, draw ends through lp on hook. Pull to tighten. Pull to tighten.

Fringe in every other st around bottom edge. ■

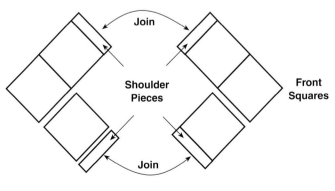

Fig. 1
Gold Nugget Cocktail Cover-Up Diagram

COZY CAFÉ AU LAIT SHRUG CONTINUED FROM PAGE 63

First Sleeve Shaping

Row 26 (WS): Holding row 25 to opposite side of foundation ch of row 1, working through both thicknesses, ch 1, sc in each of next 36 sts across edge, fasten off. *(36 sc)*

2nd Sleeve Shaping

Row 26 (WS): Working on opposite end of Shrug Body, holding row 25 to opposite side of foundation ch of row 1, join yarn in first st, ch 1, sc in same st as beg ch-1, sc in each of next 35 sts, fasten off, turn Shrug RS out. *(36 sc)*

Cuff

Rnd 1 (RS): Attach yarn in row 26 of Sleeve Shaping, ch 1, sc in side edge of row 26, work 1 sc in side edge of each row, join in beg sc, turn. *(26 sc)*

Rnd 2 (WS): Ch 3, dc in each sc around, join in 3rd ch of beg ch-3, turn.

Rnd 3 (RS): Ch 1, sc in same st as beg ch-1, **fpdc** *(see Stitch Guide)* around next sc, [sc in next sc, fpdc around next sc] around, join in beg sc, do not turn.

Rnds 4–6 (RS): Ch 1, [sc in sc, fpdc around fpdc directly below] around, join in beg sc.

At the end of rnd 6, fasten off. Rep on opposite Sleeve Shaping. ∎

RUFFLED SHOULDER WRAP CONTINUED FROM PAGE 66

For Sizes Large, X-Large, 2X-Large & 3X-Large Only

Rnd [23, 24, 25, 25]: [Rep rnd 22 [23, 24, 24] 1 [1, 1, 2, 2] times or as many rnds as needed for desired length.

For All Sizes

Rnds 19–23 [20–23, 22–25, 24–27, 25–28, 27–30, 27–30]: Sl st in center of next ch sp, ch 1, sc in same ch sp, ch 6, [sc in center of next ch sp, ch 6] around, join in beg sc. At the end of last rep, fasten off.

Button

Rnd 1: Ch 2, 8 sc in 2nd ch from hook, do not join, work in continuous rnds. *(6 sc)*

Rnd 2: 2 sc in each sc around. *(16 sc)*

Rnd 3: Rep rnd 2. *(32 sc)*

Rnds 4–8: Sc in each sc around. At the end of last rep,

sl st in next st, leaving a length of yarn, fasten off. Weave rem length through rnd 8, insert button into opening and draw opening closed, knot to secure, sew Button to left edge.

Fold ¼ of top edge of Wrap backwards and use natural sp on opposite edge for buttonhole.
Leave Wrap buttoned and pull over your head or unbutton and button as desired. ■

COOL CLASS DRESS AND SHOULDER COVER CONTINUED FROM PAGE 75

Rnd 5: Ch 1, reverse sc in each st around, join in beg sc, fasten off.
Rep on other Armhole.

SHOULDER COVER

First Half

Row 1: Beg at center back with size N hook and crystallite cream, ch 36 [36, 40], dc in 4th ch from hook, [ch 2, sk next 2 chs, dc in each of next 2 chs] 8 [8, 9] times, turn. *(18 [18, 20] dc)*

Row 2: Ch 3 *(counts as first dc)*, dc in next dc, [ch 2, dc in each of next 2 dc] across, turn.

Rep row 2 until First Half is 8 [9, 10] inches long, ending with a RS row, place a marker at each end of last row, turn.

Shaping

Row 1: Ch 3, dc in next dc, ch 1, dc in each of next 2 dc, [ch 2, dc in each of next 2 dc] 6 [6, 7] times, ch 1, dc in next 2 dc, turn.

Row 2: Ch 3, dc in next dc, sk next ch-1 sp, dc in each of next 2 dc, ch 2, [dc in each of next 2 dc, ch 2] 5 [5, 6] times, dc in each of next 2 dc, sk next ch-1 sp, dc in each of next 2 dc, turn. *(18 [18, 20] dc)*

Row 3: Ch 3, dc in each of next 2 dc, sk next dc, ch 2, [dc in each of next 2 dc, ch 2] 5 [5, 6] times, turn. *(16 [16, 18] dc)*

Row 4: Ch 3, dc in next dc, sk next dc, ch 2, [dc in each of next 2 dc, ch 2] 5 [5, 6] times, turn. *(14 [14, 16] dc)*

Row 5: Ch 3, dc in next dc, ch 1, dc in each of next 2 dc, [ch 2, dc in each of next 2 dc] 4 [4, 5] times, turn. *(14 [14, 16] dc)*

Row 6: Ch 3, dc in next dc, sk next ch-1 sp, dc in each of next 2 dc, ch 2, [dc in each of next 2 dc, ch 2] 3 [3, 4] times, dc in each of next 2 dc, sk next ch-1 sp, dc in

each of next 2 dc, fasten off. *(14 [14, 16] dc)*

2nd Half

Row 1: Beg at center back in opposite side of foundation ch of First Half, with size N hook, attach crystallite cream in first ch, ch 3, dc in next ch, [ch 2, sk next 2 chs, dc in each of next 2 chs] 8 [8, 9] times, turn. *(18 [18, 20] dc)*

Rep row 2 until 2nd Half is 8 [9, 10] inches long, ending with a RS row, place a marker at each end of last row, turn.

Shaping

Rows 1–6: Rep rows 1–6 of First Half Shaping.

Finishing

Sew rows 1–5 of Shaping tog at each end of Shoulder Cover. ■

& MORE

More is never too much when dressing up your wardrobe with stylish fashions and chic accessories. From fun jewelry, sparkling scarves and head-turning hats to dazzling purses, jazzy vests and classic tops, you'll want to make them all to maximize your style!

SLEEVELESS SHORTY VEST

DESIGN BY DARLA SIMS

INTERMEDIATE

Finished Sizes

Instructions given fit 32–34-inch bust *(small)*; changes for 36–38-inch bust *(medium)*, 40–42-inch bust *(large)* and 44–46-inch bust *(X-large)* are in [ ].

Finished Garment Measurements

Bust: 36½ inches *(small)* [40 inches *(medium)*, 44½ inches *(large)*, 50 inches *(X-large)*]

Gauge

Size H hook: 4 sc = 1 inch; 4 rows = 1 inch
Size I hook: 6 dc = 2 inches
Size K hook: 5 dc = 2 inches; 4 dc rows = 3 inches

Pattern Note

Weave in loose ends as work progresses.

VEST

BACK

Ribbing

Row 1: With size H hook, ch 8, sc in 2nd ch from hook,

Materials

6 SUPER BULKY

• Red Heart Bijou super bulky (super chunky) weight yarn (1¾ oz/84 yds/50g per ball): 6 [7, 8, 9] balls #3638 peridot
• Sizes H/8/5mm, I/9/5.5mm and K/10½/6.5mm crochet hooks or sizes needed to obtain gauge
• Yarn needle
• 1⅝-inch pendants: 2

sc in each rem ch across, turn. *(7 sc)*
Row 2: Ch 1, working in **back lp** *(see Stitch Guide)* of each st, sc in each st across, turn. *(7 sc)*
Rows 3–46 [3–50, 3–56, 3–60]: Rep row 2.

Body

Row 1: With size I hook, working across side edge of Ribbing rows, ch 3 *(counts as first dc)*, work 45 [49, 55, 59] dc across, turn. *(46 [50, 56, 60] dc)*
Row 2: With size K hook, ch 3, dc in each dc across, turn.
Rows 3–9: Ch 3, dc in each dc across, turn. At the end of row 9, fasten off.

Armhole Shaping

Row 10: Sk first 5 [5, 7, 8] sts, attach yarn to next st, ch 3, dc in each dc across to last 5 [5, 7, 8] sts, leaving these sts unworked, turn. *(36 [40, 42, 44] dc)*
Row 11: Ch 3, dc in each dc across, turn.
Rows 12–20 [12–20, 12–22, 12–22]: Rep row 11. At the end of last rep, fasten off.

Left Front

Ribbing

Row 1: Rep row 1 of Back Ribbing. *(7 sc)*
Rows 2–22 [2–24, 2–28, 2–30]: Rep row 2 of Back Ribbing.

Body

Row 1: With size I hook, working across side edge of Ribbing rows, ch 3, work 22 [24, 27, 29] dc across, turn. *(23 [25, 28, 30] dc)*

Row 2: With size K hook, ch 3, dc in each dc across, turn.

Row 3: Ch 3, dc in each dc across to last 2 dc, **dc dec** *(see Stitch Guide)* in next 2 dc, turn. *(22 [24, 27, 29] dc)*

Row 4: Ch 3, dc in each dc across, turn.

Rows 5–8: [Rep rows 3 and 4 alternately] twice. *(20 [22, 25, 27] dc)*

Row 9: Rep row 3. *(19 [21, 24, 26] dc)*

Armhole Shaping

Row 10: Ch 3, dc in each dc across to last 5 [5, 7, 8] dc, leaving rem sts unworked, turn. *(14 [16, 17, 18] dc)*

Row 11: Ch 3, dc across to last 2 dc, dc dec in next 2 dc, turn. *(13 [15, 16, 17] dc)*

Row 12: Ch 3, dc in each dc across, turn.

Rows 13–16: [Rep rows 11 and 12 alternately] twice. *(11 [13, 14, 15] dc)*

Row 17: Rep row 11. *(10 [12, 13, 14] dc)*

For Sizes Small & Medium Only

Rows 18–20: Rep row 12. At the end of last rep, fasten off.

For Sizes Large & X-Large Only

Row 18: Rep row 12.

Row 19: Rep row 11. *([12, 13] dc)*

Rows 20–22: Rep row 12. At the end of last rep, fasten off.

Right Front

Ribbing

Rows 1–22 [1–24, 1–28, 1–30]: Rep rows 1–22 [1–24, 1–28, 1–30] of Back Ribbing rows.

Body

Row 1: With size I hook, working across side edge of Ribbing rows, ch 3, work 22 [24, 27, 29] dc across, turn. *(23 [25, 28, 30] dc)*

Row 2: With size K hook, ch 3, dc in each dc across, turn.

Row 3: Ch 3, dc dec in next 2 sts, dc in each rem dc across, turn. *(22 [24, 27, 29] dc)*

Row 4: Ch 3, dc in each dc across, turn.

Rows 5–8: [Rep rows 3 and 4 alternately] twice. *(20 [22, 25, 27] dc)*

Row 9: Rep row 3, fasten off. *(19 [21, 24, 26] dc)*

Shape Armhole

Row 10: Sk first 5 [5, 7, 8] dc, attach yarn in next dc, ch 3, dc in each rem dc across, turn. *(14 [16, 17, 18] dc)*

Row 11: Ch 3, dc dec in next 2 sts, dc in each rem dc across, turn. *(13 [15, 16, 17] dc)*

Row 12: Ch 3, dc in each dc across, turn.

Rows 13–16: [Rep rows 11 and 12 alternately] twice. *(11 [13, 14, 15] dc)*

Row 17: Rep row 11. *(10 [12, 13, 14] dc)*

For Sizes Small & Medium Only

Rows 18–20: Rep row 12. At the end of last rep, fasten off.

For Sizes Large & X-Large Only

Row 18: Rep row 12.

Row 19: Rep row 11. *([12, 13] dc)*

Rows 20–22: Rep row 12. At the end of last rep, fasten off.

Assembly

Sew shoulder and side seams.

Collar

Row 1: With size I hook, attach yarn at lower Right Front, ch 1, work 44 [44, 46, 46] sc to shoulder seam, 16 [16, 18, 18] sc across Back, 44 [44, 46, 46] sc from shoulder seam to lower Left Front, turn, fasten off. *(104 [104, 110, 110] sc)*

Row 2: Sk first 12 sc, attach yarn with sc in next sc, sc in each of next 31 [31, 33, 33] sc, 2 sc in next st at shoulder seam, sc across Back neck, 2 sc in next st at shoulder seam, sc in each of next 32 [32, 34, 34] sc down Left Front, leaving last 12 sts unworked, turn. *(82 [82, 87, 87] sc)*

Row 3: With size K hook, ch 1, sc in each of next 2 sc, ch 3, sk next 2 sc, sc in next sc, [ch 2, sk next sc, sc in next sc, ch 3, sk next 2 sc, sc in next sc] across, ending with sc in next sc, turn.

Row 4: Ch 3, dc in first st, ch 2, sc in next ch-3 sp, ch 2, [3 dc in next ch-2 sp, ch 2, sc in next ch-3 sp, ch 2] across, ending with 2 dc in last st, turn.

Row 5: Ch 3, sc in next ch-2 sp, [ch 2, sc in next ch-2 sp, ch 3, sc in next ch-2 sp] across, ending with ch 1, hdc in last st, turn.

Row 6: Ch 3, 3 dc in next ch-2 sp, [ch 2, sc in next ch-3 sp, ch 2, 3 dc in next ch-2 sp] across, ending with ch 2, sc in last st, turn.

Row 7: Ch 2, sc in next ch-2 sp, [ch 3, sc in next ch-2 sp, ch 2, sc in next ch-2 sp] across, ending with hdc in last st, turn.

Row 8: Ch 3, dc in same st as beg ch-3, ch 2 [sc in next ch-3 sp, ch 2, 3 dc in next ch-2 sp, ch 2] across, ending with 2 dc in last st, turn.

Rows 9–12: Rep rows 5–8. Fasten off.

Tie

Make 2.

For each tie, cut 1 length 2 yds long and thread through pendant, with pendant at center, fold yarn in half lengthwise. Form a slip knot close to pendant, ch 12, fasten off.

Sew a tie to first sc of row 2 of Collar at each side of front opening. ∎

HOT PANTS SET

DESIGNS BY JOYCE BRAGG

INTERMEDIATE

Finished Sizes

Instructions given fit woman's
X-small; changes for small,
medium, large and X-large
are in [ ].

Finished Garment
Measurements

Top: Empire waist: 27 inches
(X-small) [28 inches (small),
29 inches (medium), 30
inches (large), 31 inches
(X-large)]

Shorts: Hip (unstretched):
27 inches (X-small) [29
inches (small), 31 inches
(medium), 32 inches (large),
33 inches (X-large)]

Gauge

Size G hook: 5 sc = 1 inch; 5 sc rows = 1 inch

Pattern Notes

Weave in loose ends as work progresses.
Join rounds with a slip stitch unless otherwise stated.
Top is loose fitting, designed to wear over a tank or t-shirt.

Special Stitch

Block stitch (block st): At the beg of a row, ch 3 (counts
as first dc), within a row or rnd replace ch-3 with a dc,
*dc in next st, [insert hook over vertical post of last dc,

Materials

• Berroco Suede
bulky (chunky)
weight yarn (1¾ oz/120
yds/50g per ball):
    6 balls #3753 Belle Star
    1 ball #3737 Roy Rodgers
• Sizes F/5/3.75mm and
G/6/4mm crochet hooks or
size needed to obtain gauge
• Tapestry needle
• Stitch markers

yo, draw up a lp] 3 times, yo, draw through all 4 lps on
hook, dc in next st, rep from * as indicated.

SHORTS

First Leg

Rnd 1: With size G hook and pink, ch 73 [78, 83, 88, 91],
sc in 2nd ch from hook, sc in each rem ch across, taking
care not to twist, join in first sc. (72 [77, 82, 87, 90] sc)

Rnd 2: Work **block st** (see Special Stitch), place marker
on first block st, block st around, join in 3rd ch of
beg ch-3.

Rnd 3: Ch 1, working in **back lps** (see Stitch Guide), sc in
each st around, join in beg sc, fasten off. (72 [77, 82, 87,
90] sts)

2nd Leg

Rnds 1–3: Rep rnds 1–3 of First Leg, do not fasten off
at the end of rnd 3.

Joining

Rnd 4: Ch 1, working in back lps, sc in each of next 34
[36, 38, 40, 42] sts, sc in 3rd st on first leg and in each of
next 67 [71, 75, 79, 83] sts, leaving 4 [5, 5, 6, 6] sc free
for crotch, sk next 4 [5, 5, 6, 6] sts on 2nd leg for crotch,
sc in next sc and in each of next 33 [35, 37, 39, 41] sts,
join in beg sc, place marker. (136 [144, 153, 161, 165] sts)

Upper Shorts

Rnds 1 & 2: Ch 1, working in back lps only, sc in each st
around, join in beg sc.

Rnd 3: Work block st in next 3 sts (hip area), sc in each of
next 66 [70, 74, 78, 82] sts, block st in next 3 sts (hip area),

sc in each rem st around, join in 3rd ch of beg ch-3.

Rnd 4: Ch 1, sc in each st around, join in beg sc.

Short row: With a separate ball of pink, attach in 8th st from block st, sc in each of next 53 [57, 61, 74, 78] sts, sl st in next st, turn, sl st in first sc, sc in each of next 51 [55, 59, 72, 76] sts, fasten off.

Rnd 5: Block st in same 3 sts as block st below, sc in each of next 67 [71, 75, 79, 83] sts, block st in same 3 sts as block st below, sc in each rem st around, join in 3rd ch of beg ch-3.

Rep rnds 4 and 6 alternately until piece measures 3 [3½, 4, 4, 4½] inches from crotch, fasten off.

Front Opening

Row 1: With WS facing, attach pink in **front lp** (see Stitch Guide) of 41st [43rd, 45th, 47th, 49th] st from center of block st of hip area, ch 1, sc in front lp of same st as beg ch-1, sc in front lp of each st to last 4 sts, turn.

Row 2: Ch 1, working in front lps, sc in each st, turn. Rep row 2 until piece measures 7 [7½, 8, 8½, 9] inches from crotch, ending on WS, fasten off.

Row 3: Working another short row, with RS facing, attach pink in 36th [38th, 40th, 42nd, 44th] st, working in front lps only, ch 1, sc in each of next 75 [77, 79, 81, 83] sts across back of shorts, turn.

Row 4: Sl st in first st, sc in front lp of each of next 75 [77, 79, 81, 83] sts, sl st in next st, fasten off.

Row 5: Attach pink in first sc st before previous short rows, ch 1, working in front lps only, sc in each st across, turn.

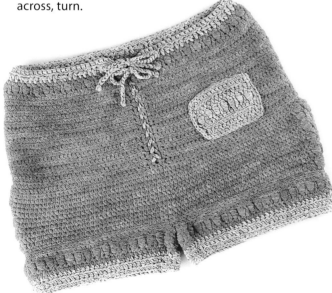

Rows 6–8: Ch 1, working in front lps only, sc in each st across, turn.

Row 9: Ch 3, work block st, [sk next st, block st] across, turn.

Row 10: Ch 1, sc in each st across, working around front opening, sc evenly spaced down front opening and up opposite edge, join in beg sc, fasten off.

Waistline Trim

Row 11: With RS facing, attach beige, ch 2 (counts as first hdc), hdc in each sc of row 10, turn.

Row 12: Ch 1, working in front lps only, sc in each st across, fasten off.

Lower Leg Border

Rnd 1: With RS facing, attach beige in opposite side of foundation ch of Leg, ch 2, hdc in each st around, join in 2nd ch of beg ch-2.

Rnd 2: Ch 2, hdc in each st around, join in 2nd ch of beg ch-2.

Rnd 3: Ch 1, working in back lps only, sc in each st around, join in beg sc, fasten off.

Rep on opposite Leg.

Front Closure

With size F hook and beige, crochet a ch 15 [15, 16, 17, 17] inches, fasten off and lace ch through the sc on each side of opening. Beg at bottom corners, sk 2 sts between each lacing, ending at last sc row of pink color, tie ends in a bow.

Drawstring

With size F hook and beige, crochet a ch approximately 30 inches or to length desired to fit Shorts size. Starting at center back, weave ch through hdc sts of row 11 of Waistline Trim, draw ends up, tie in a bow and let it fall over bow of Front Closure.

Pocket

Row 1: Beg at bottom, with size F hook and beige, ch 16, sc in 2nd ch from hook, sc in each rem ch across, turn. (15 sc)

Row 2: Ch 2, hdc in each st across, turn.

Row 3: Block st across row, turn.

Row 4: Ch 1, sc in each st across, turn.

Row 5: Rep row 2.

Row 6: Ch 2, working in back lps only, hdc in each st across, turn.

Note: For larger Pocket, continue to rep row 6 to desired width.

Row 7: Ch 1, working down side edge of rows, sc evenly spaced in opposite side of foundation ch, 2 sc in corner, sc in each ch across, 2 sc in corner, sc in each st up opposite edge, sl st in next st, leaving a length of yarn, fasten off.

Sew Pocket to front left side of Pants.

TOP

Body

Foundation row: With size G hook and pink, ch 137 [142, 147, 152, 157] sc in 2nd ch from hook, sc in each rem ch across, turn. *(136 [141, 146, 151, 156] sts)*

Row 1: With size F hook, work block st across, turn.

Row 2: With size G hook, working in front lps only, ch 1, sc in each st across, turn. *(136 [141, 146, 151, 156] sts)*

Row 3: Ch 1, sc in each st across, turn.

Row 4: Ch 1, working in front lps only, sc in each st across, turn.

Rows 5–12: [Rep rows 3 and 4 alternately] 4 times. At the end of last rep, fasten off.

Short Front Rows

Row 1: With size G hook, attach a separate ball of pink with sl st in 6th sc from beg, working in both lps, sc in each of next 20 [25, 25, 25, 30] sts, sl st in next st, turn, sc in each of next 20 [20, 30, 35, 35] sts, draw up a lp, drop yarn.

Row 1: With size G hook, attach a separate ball of pink with sl st in 6th sc of opposite side, sc in both lps of each of next 20 [25, 25, 25, 30] sts, sl st in next st, turn, sc in each of next 20 [20, 30, 35, 35] sts, fasten off.

Row 2: With RS facing, attach pink in first st, ch 1, sc in each st across, turn.

Rows 3 & 4: Ch 1, sc in each st across, turn.

Left Front Armhole

Row 1: Ch 1, sk first st, sc in each of next 15 [15, 20, 25, 25] sts, 2 sc in next st, sc in each of next 18 [18, 23, 28, 28] sts, turn.

For Sizes X-Small, Small & Medium Only

Row 2: Ch 1, sc in each of next 18 [18, 23] sts, 2 sc in next sc, sc in each rem sc across, turn.

Row 3: Ch 1, sc in each of next 15 [15, 20] sts, 2 sc in next st, sc in next st, 2 sc in next st, sc across to armhole, turn.

For Sizes Large & X-Large Only

Row 2: Ch 1, sc in each of next 28 [28] sts, 2 sc in next st, sc in each rem st across, turn.

Row 3: Ch 1, sc in each st to within 1 st before inc on previous row, 2 sc in next st, sc in next st, 2 sc in next st, sc in each rem sc across to armhole, turn.

For All Sizes

Row 4: Sk first sc at armhole, sc in each st to within 1 st before inc of previous row, inc 1 st in sc on each side of inc sts on previous row, sc in rem sc sts across, turn.

Row 5: Ch 1, sc in each st to within 1 st before inc on previous row, inc 1 st on each side of inc on previous row, sc in each rem sc across, turn.

Rows 6–10: Ch 1, sc in each sc across, turn. Ending with last rep at front edge, turn.

CONTINUED ON PAGE 164

KIWI VEST & HEADBAND

DESIGNS BY JOYCE BRAGG

INTERMEDIATE

Finished Sizes

Vest: Bust: Instructions given
fit 32–34-inch bust *(small)*;
changes for 36–38-inch bust
(medium) and 40–42-inch
bust *(large)* are in [ ].
Headband: 18½ inches,
excluding ties

Finished Garment Measurements

Bust: 32 inches *(small)*
[36 inches *(medium)*,
40 inches *(large)*]

Gauge

Size F hook *(small)*: 14 sts = 5 inches; 4 rows = 1 inch
Size G hook *(medium)*: 18 sts = 4 inches; 5 rows = 1 inch
Size H hook *(large)*: 20 sts = 4 inches; 6 rows = 1 inch

Pattern Notes

Weave in loose ends as work progresses.
Join rounds with a slip stitch unless otherwise stated.
Row 3 establishes the Vest pattern.

VEST

Right Front

Foundation row: Beg at shoulder, with size F [G, H]
hook, ch 16, sl st in 2nd ch from hook, sl st in each rem
ch across, turn.
Row 1: Ch 1, [hdc in next st, sl st loosely in next st]
across, turn. *(15 sts)*
Row 2: Ch 2 *(counts as first hdc)*, sk first sl st, working in

Materials

- TLC Cotton
  Plus medium
  (worsted) weight yarn (3½
  oz/178 yds/100g per ball):
    3 balls #3643 kiwi
- Sizes F/5/3.75mm, G/6/4mm
  and H/8/5mm crochet
  hooks or sizes needed to
  obtain gauge
- Tapestry needle

4 MEDIUM

back lp *(see Stitch Guide)* of each st across, [sl st loosely
in next hdc, hdc in next sl st] across, turn. *(15 sts)*
Row 3: Ch 1, working in back lps only, [hdc in sl st, sl st
loosely in hdc] across, turn.
Rows 4–11: [Rep rows 2 and 3] 4 times.
Row 12: Rep row 2.

Neck & Armhole Shaping

Row 13: Maintaining pattern of row 3 in back lps only,
hdc in sl st and sl st loosely in hdc, work 2 sts in first st,
work in pattern across, turn. *(16 sts)*
Rep row 13 until Front measures 6½ inches from first
inc, ending at armhole edge, turn. *(31 sts)*
Row 14: At armhole edge, ch 13, sl st in 2nd ch from
hook, sl st in each ch, sl st loosely in last st made before
ch-13, continue in pattern across, to last 2 sts, **dec 1 st**
(see Stitch Guide) in last 2 sts, turn.
Row 15: Work in pattern of row 3 across, turn.
Row 16: Work in pattern of row 3 across, dec 1 st in last
2 sts, turn.
Rep rows 15 and 16 until armhole measures 3 inches,
ending at armhole edge, do not work last st and turn-
ing ch, turn.
Row 17: Maintaining pattern of row 3, dec 1 st at beg
and end of row, turn.
Row 18: Work even in pattern of row 3 across, turn.
Rep rows 17 and 18 until 3 sts rem.
Row 19: Ch 2, sk 1 st, hdc in last st, fasten off.

Left Front

Work Left Front same as Right Front, pattern is reversed.

Back

Make 2.

Foundation row: Beg at shoulder, with size F [G, H]

CONTINUED ON PAGE 165

LADDER-STITCH CLOCHE

DESIGN BY KATHERINE ENG

BEGINNER

Finished Size

Adult

Finished Garment Measurements

Bottom circumference =
22 inches

Materials

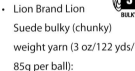

- Lion Brand Lion
  Suede bulky (chunky)
  weight yarn (3 oz/122 yds/
  85g per ball):
    1½ oz/61 yds/43g
    #126 coffee
    ½ oz/20 yds/14g each
    #132 olive and #147
    eggplant
- Size H/8/5mm crochet hook or
  size needed to obtain gauge
- Tapestry needle

Gauge

First 2 rnds = 1½ inches

Pattern Notes

Weave in loose ends as work progresses.
Join rounds with a slip stitch unless otherwise stated.
For smaller size, use size G hook.

CLOCHE

Rnd 1: With coffee, ch 4, join in first ch to form a ring, ch 1, 8 sc in ring, join in beg sc. *(8 sc)*

Rnd 2: Ch 1, (sc, ch 2, sc) in each sc around, join in beg sc. *(8 ch-2 sps)*

Rnd 3: Sl st into ch-2 sp, ch 1, (sc, ch 2, sc) in same ch-2 sp, ch 1, [(sc, ch 2, sc) in next ch-2 sp, ch 1] around, join in beg sc.

Rnd 4: Sl st into ch-2 sp, ch 1, (sc, ch 2, sc) in same ch-2 sp, (sc, ch 2, sc) in next ch-1 sp, [(sc, ch 2, sc) in next ch-2 sp, (sc, ch 2, sc) in next ch-1 sp] around, join in beg sc. *(16 ch-2 sps)*

Rnd 5: Sl st into ch-2 sp, ch 1, (sc, ch 2, sc) in same ch-2 sp and in each rem ch-2 sp around, join in beg sc.

Rnd 6: Rep rnd 3.

Rnd 7: Sl st into ch-2 sp, ch 1, (sc, ch 2, sc) in same ch-2 sp, ch 2, [(sc, ch 2, sc) in next ch-2 sp, ch 2] around, join in beg sc.

Rnd 8: Sl st into ch-2 sp, ch 1, (sc, ch 2, sc) in same ch-2 sp, ch 2, sk next ch-2 sp, [(sc, ch 2, sc) in next ch-2 sp, ch 2, sk next ch-2 sp] around, join in beg sc.

Rnd 9: Sl st into ch-2 sp, ch 1, (sc, ch 2, sc) in same ch-2 sp, ch 3, sk next ch-2 sp, [(sc, ch 2, sc) in next ch-2 sp, ch 3, sk next ch-2 sp] around, join in beg sc.

Rnd 10: Sl st into next ch-2 sp, ch 1, (sc, ch 2, sc) in same ch-2 sp, ch 3, sk next ch-3 sp, [(sc, ch 2, sc) in next ch-2 sp, ch 3, sk next ch-3 sp] around, join in beg sc.

Rnds 11 & 12: Rep rnd 10. At the end of rnd 12, fasten off.

Rnd 13: Draw up a lp of olive in first ch-2 sp of previous rnd, ch 1, rep rnd 10, fasten off.

Rnd 14: Draw up a lp of eggplant in first ch-2 sp of previous rnd, ch 1, rep rnd 10, fasten off.

Rnd 15: Rep rnd 13.

Rnd 16: Draw up a lp of coffee in first ch-2 sp of previous rnd, ch 1, (sc, ch 2, sc) in same ch-2 sp, ch 2, sk next ch-3 sp, [(sc, ch 2, sc) in next ch-2 sp, ch 2, sk next ch-3 sp] around, join in beg sc.

CONTINUED ON PAGE 166

STARLIGHT SCARF

DESIGN BY SUE CHILDRESS

EASY

Finished Size

2¼ x 42 inches

Materials

- Tahki Star light (DK) weight yarn (163 yds/20g ball): 1 ball #19 Sagittarius
- Berroco Softwist medium (worsted) weight yarn (1¾ oz/100 yds/50g per hank): 1 hank #9443 smoothie
- Size I/9/5.5mm crochet hook or size needed to obtain gauge
- Tapestry needle
- Ornamental pin (optional)

Gauge

With 1 strand of each held tog: 2 dc and ch-2 = 1 inch

SCARF

Row 1: With 1 strand each held tog, ch 156, dc in 4th ch from hook, [ch 2, sk next 2 chs, dc in each of next 2 chs] across, turn. *(39 groups 2-dc, 38 ch-2 sps)*

Row 2: Ch 3 *(counts as first dc)*, 2 sc in next ch-2 sp, [ch 2, 2 sc in next ch-2 sp] across, ending with dc in last dc, turn.

Row 3: Ch 3, dc in same dc as beg ch-3, [ch 2, 2 dc in next ch-2 sp] across, ending with 2 dc in last dc, turn.

Row 4: Ch 6, working in dc of row 1, [sk 2 sc of row 2, sc in first dc of next 2-dc group of row 1, ch 6] across, ending with sc in top of first dc of row 3, turn.

Row 5: Rep row 2.

Row 6: Rep row 3.

Row 7: Ch 6, working in dc of row 3, [sk 2 sc of row 5, sc in first dc of next 2-dc group of row 3, ch 6] across, ending with sc in top of first dc of row 6, **do not turn**.

Row 8: Working in ends of Scarf rows, [ch 6, sc in end of next row] 5 times, fasten off.

Row 9: Working in opposite end of Scarf rows, attach 1 strand each in row end, ch 1, sc in same row, [ch 6, sc in next row] 5 times, fasten off.

Finishing

Pass end of Scarf through ch-2 sp of row 3 approximately 6 inches up from opposite end of scarf, secure with pin. ∎

MOONLIGHT MAGIC

DESIGN BY JOHANNA DZIKOWSKI

EASY

Finished Size

7 inches square, excluding
Shoulder Strap

Gauge

5 dc = 2 inches

Pattern Notes

Weave in loose ends as work progresses.

Join rounds with a slip stitch unless otherwise stated.

EVENING BAG

Flap

Rnd 1: With glacier bay, ch 6, join in first ch to form a ring, ch 1, [sc in ring, ch 3] 12 times, join in beg sc. *(12 ch-3 sps)*

Materials

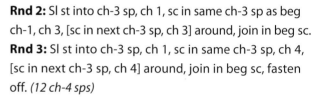

- Lion Brand Moonlight Mohair bulky (chunky) weight yarn (1¾ oz/82 yds/50g per skein):
    1 skein #205 glacier bay
- Lion Brand Chenille Thick & Quick super bulky (super chunky) weight yarn (3 oz/100 yds/80g per skein):
    20 yds #111 midnight blue
- Size I/9/5.5mm crochet hooks or size needed to obtain gauge
- Tapestry needle

Rnd 2: Sl st into ch-3 sp, ch 1, sc in same ch-3 sp as beg ch-1, ch 3, [sc in next ch-3 sp, ch 3] around, join in beg sc.

Rnd 3: Sl st into ch-3 sp, ch 1, sc in same ch-3 sp, ch 4, [sc in next ch-3 sp, ch 4] around, join in beg sc, fasten off. *(12 ch-4 sps)*

Rnd 4: Attach dark blue in any ch-4 sp, ch 1, sc in same ch-4 sp, ch 5, [sc in next ch-4 sp, ch 5] around, join in beg sc. *(12 ch-5 sps)*

Rnd 5: Ch 1, [8 hdc in next ch-5 sp, sc in next ch-5 sp] around, join in first hdc, fasten off. *(48 hdc, 6 sc)*

Body

Row 1: With glacier bay, ch 19, sc in 2nd ch from hook, sc in each rem ch across, turn. *(18 sc)*

Row 2: Ch 1, dc in each sc across, turn.

Row 3: Ch 1, dc in each dc across, turn.

Rows 4–18: Rep row 3.

Row 19: Ch 1, sc in each dc across, leaving a length of yarn, fasten off.

Holding row 1 and row 19 of Body tog for top opening, with rem length of yarn, sew each side seam.

Shoulder Strap

Note: *Roll remainder of glacier bay into 2 equal balls.*

Row 1: Attach first ball of glacier bay in sewn side seam, ch 1, 3 sc in same st, turn. *(3 sc)*

Row 2: Ch 1, hdc in each sc across, turn. *(3 hdc)*

Row 3: Ch 1, hdc in each hdc across, turn.

Rows 4–17: Rep row 3. At the end of row 17, fasten off.

Row 18: Attach midnight blue in first hdc, ch 1, hdc in

each hdc across, turn.

Row 19: Ch 1, hdc in each hdc across, turn.
Rep row 19 until Strap reaches desired length or until dark blue is gone.

Row 20: Attach glacier bay to last row of dark blue, ch 1, hdc in each of next 3 hdc, turn.

Rows 21–35: Rep row 3.

Row 36: Ch 1, work 3 sc in opposite side seam, fasten off. ∎

EARTH CHILD

DESIGNS BY MARY JANE HALL

EASY

Finished Sizes

Choker: 7/8 x 13¼ inches

Bracelet: 7 inches in diameter

Materials

- Aunt Lydia's "Denim" Quick 8-ply crochet medium (worsted) weight thread (400 yds per ball):
    200 yds #1021 linen
- Size E/4/3.5mm crochet hook or size needed to obtain gauge
- Yarn needle
- ¾-inch metal rings: 7
- 1¼-inch metal ring: 1
- 18mm wooden oval beads: 3
- 28mm wooden oval beads: 4
- 15mm button: 1

Gauge

3 sc = 1 inch

Pattern Notes

Weave in loose ends as work progresses.

Join rounds with a slip stitch unless otherwise stated.

If larger Bracelet is desired add one 1¼-inch metal ring and one 28mm wooden bead for a 2-inch increase in diameter.

CHOKER

Neckband

Row 1: Ch 5, sc in 2nd ch from hook, sc in each rem ch across, turn. *(4 sc)*

Row 2: Ch 1, sc in each sc across, turn.

Rows 3–69: Rep row 2. If longer choker is desired, add needed number of rows.

Buttonhole

Row 70: Ch 5, sk first 3 sc, sl st in 4th sc, turn.

Row 71: Work 7 sc over ch-5 sp, sl st in side edge of row 69, fasten off.

Large Ring

Rnd 1: Attach linen to 1¼-inch metal ring, ch 1, work 30 sc over metal ring, join in beg sc, leaving a length of cotton, fasten off. *(30 sc)*

CONTINUED ON PAGE 167

GRANNY SQUARE SHRINK VEST

DESIGN BY MARTY MILLER

EASY

Finished Sizes

Instructions given fit 28–30-inch bust (X-small); changes for 32–34-inch bust (small), 36–38-inch bust (medium), 40–42-inch bust (large) and 44–46-inch bust (X-large) are in [ ].

Finished Garment Measurements

Bust: 27 inches (X-small) [31 inches (small), 35 inches (medium), 49 inches (large), 43 inches (X-large)]

Length: 14½ inches (X-small) [16½ inches (small), 18 inches (medium), 19½ inches (large), 20½ inches (X-large)]

Gauge

Rnds 1 and 2 = 4 inches; 5 dc = 2 inches

Pattern Notes

Weave in loose ends as work progresses.

Join rounds with a slip stitch unless otherwise stated.

Materials

• Lion Brand Lion Suede bulky (chunky) weight yarn (3 oz/122 yds/85g per skein): 2 [3, 3, 4, 5] skeins #110 denim
• Size J/10/6mm crochet hook or size needed to obtain gauge
• Tapestry needle
• Stitch markers

VEST

Body

Make 2.

Rnd 1: Ch 6, join in first ch of ch-6, ch 3 (counts as first dc), 15 dc in ring, join in 3rd ch of beg ch-3. (16 dc)

Rnd 2: Ch 3, dc in same st as beg ch-3, 2 dc in each dc around, join in 3rd ch of beg ch-3. (32 dc)

Rnd 3: Ch 5 (counts as first dc, ch-2), sk next dc, [dc in next dc, ch 2, sk next dc] around, join in 3rd ch of beg ch-5. (16 dc, 16 ch-2 sps)

CONTINUED ON PAGE 167

SWEATER FOR A SPECIAL EVENING

DESIGN BY DARLA SIMS

INTERMEDIATE

Finished Sizes

Instructions given fit 32-24-inch bust *(small)*; changes for 36-38-inch bust *(medium)*, 40-42-inch bust *(large)*, 44-46-inch bust *(X-large)*, 48-50-inch bust *(2X-large)* and 52-54-inch bust *(3X-large)* are in [ ].

Finished Garment Measurements

Bust: 36 inches *(small)* [40 inches *(medium)*, 44 inches *(large)*, 48 inches, *(X-large)*, 50 inches *(2X-large)*, 56 inches *(3X-large)*]

Gauge

Size G hook: 5 sc = 1 inch; 5 sc back lp rows = 1 inch
Size I hook: 12 pattern sts = 4 inches; 12 pattern rows = 4 inches
Take time to check gauge.

Pattern Note

To work in pattern, repeat rows 2–5 consecutively.

Materials

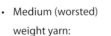

- Medium (worsted) weight yarn:
  9 [9, 12, 12, 12, 12] oz/450 [450, 600, 600, 600, 600] yds/255 [255, 340, 340, 340, 340]g copper
- Lion Brand Glitterspun medium (worsted) weight yarn (1¾ oz/115yds/50g per ball):
  5 [5, 6, 6, 7, 7] balls #135 bronze
- Sizes G/6/4mm and I/9/5.5mm crochet hooks or sizes needed to obtain gauge
- Tapestry needle

SWEATER

Back

Row 1: With size I hook and copper, ch 55 [61, 67, 73, 79, 85], sc in 2nd ch from hook, dc in next ch, [sc in next ch, dc in next ch] across, turn. *(54 [60, 66, 72, 78, 84] sts)*

Row 2: Ch 1, sc in each dc and dc in each sc across **changing colors** *(see Stitch Guide)* to bronze in last st made, turn. Drop copper. Pick up again when needed.

Row 3: Ch 1, sc in each dc and dc in each sc across, turn.

Row 4: Ch 1, sc in each dc and dc in each sc across changing to copper in last st, turn. Drop bronze. Pick up again when needed.

Row 5: Ch 1, sc in each dc and dc in each sc across, turn.

Rows 6–30: Work in pattern *(see Pattern Note)* until piece measures about 11 inches from beg, ending with row 4. At end of last row, do not change to copper. Fasten off both yarns.

Sleeves

Row 31: Join copper with sl st in last st on row 30, ch 12. Fasten off. Join copper with sl st in first st of row 30, for sleeve, ch 13, sc in 2nd ch from hook, dc in next ch, [sc in next ch, dc in next ch] across to row 30, work in pattern across to ch-12, [sc in next ch, dc in next ch] across, turn. *(78 [84, 90, 96, 102, 108] sts)*

Next rows: Work in pattern until piece measures 19 [19½, 20, 20½, 21, 21½] inches from beg. At end of last row, fasten off.

Front

Work same as back until piece measures 16 [16½, 17, 17½, 18, 18½] from beg.

First Shoulder

Row 1: Work in pattern across first 34 [36, 39, 42, 44, 46] sts, leaving rem sts unworked, turn.

Row 2: Work in pattern.

Row 3: Work in pattern across to last 2 sts, **dc dec** *(see Stitch Guide)* in last 2 sts, turn. *(33 [35, 38, 41, 43, 45] sts)*

Rows 4–9: [Rep rows 2 and 3 alternately] 3 times. *(30 [32, 35, 38, 40, 42] sts at end of last row)*

Row 10: Work in pattern. Fasten off.

2nd Shoulder

Row 1: Sk next 10 [12, 12, 12, 14, 16] sts at center front neck edge, using yarn color to maintain pattern, join with sl st in next st, ch 1, work in pattern across, turn. *(34 [36, 39, 42, 44, 46] sts)*

Row 2: Work in pattern.

Row 3: Ch 2 *(ch-2 is not used or counted as st)*, sk first st, work in pattern across, turn. *(33 [35, 38, 41, 43, 45] sts)*

Row 4: Work in pattern across leaving ch-2 unworked.

Rows 5–10: [Rep rows 3 and 4 alternately] 3 times. At end of last row, fasten off. *(30 [32, 35, 38, 40, 42] sts at end of last row)*

For shoulder seams, sew last row on each Front shoulder to 30 [32, 35, 38, 40, 42] sts to each end of last row on Back leaving center 18 [20, 20, 20, 22, 24] sts on Back open for neck edge.

Neck Ribbing

Rnd 1: With size G hook, join bronze with sc in first st after left shoulder seam, evenly sp 11 sc in ends of rows across to center front sts, sc in each of next 10 [12, 12, 12, 14, 16] sts at center front, evenly sp 12 sts in ends of row across to right shoulder seam, sc in each of next 18 [20, 20, 20, 22, 24] sts across Back neck edge, join with sl st in beg sc. *(52 [56, 56, 56, 60, 64] sc)*

Row 2: Ch 12, sc in 2nd ch from hook, sc in each ch across, sk first st on rnd 1, sl st in each of next 2 sts, turn. *(11 sc)*

Note: *Sl sts are not worked into or counted as sts.*

Row 3: Working in **back lps** *(see Stitch Guide)*, ch 1, sk sl sts, sc in each sc across, turn.

Row 4: Ch 1, sc in back lps of each sc across, sl st in both lps of each of next 2 sts on rnd 1, turn.

Rows 5 & 6: Rep rows 3 and 4.

Row 7: Rep row 3. Leaving 10-inch end for sewing, fasten off.

Matching sts, sew back lps of last row and starting ch at beg of row 2 tog to form rib.

Arm Band

Row 1: Working in ends of rows on 1 Sleeve, with size G hook and bronze, join with sc in end of first row, sc in next row, [**sc dec** *(see Stitch Guide)* in next 2 rows, sc in each of next 2 rows] across Sleeve *(last rep may not end evenly)*, turn.

Rows 2–5: Ch 1, sc in each st across, turn. At end of last row, fasten off.

Rep on other Sleeve.

Sew Sleeve and side seams.

Bottom Ribbing

Rnd 1: With RS of work facing, working on opposite side of starting ch on row 1 at bottom edge, with size G hook and copper, join with sc in first st after 1 side seam, sc in each of next 3 chs, sc dec in next 2 chs, [sc in each of next 4 chs, sc dec in next 2 chs] around Front and Back, join with sl st in beg sc, **do not turn**. *(90 [100, 110, 120, 130, 140] sts)*

Row 2: Ch 8, sc in 2nd ch from hook, sc in each ch across, sk first st on rnd 1, sl st in each of next 2 sts, turn. *(7 sc)*

Note: *Sl sts are not worked into or counted as sts.*

Row 3: Ch 1, sk sl sts, sc in back lps of each sc across, turn.

Row 4: Ch 1, sc in back lps of each sc across, sl st in both lps in each of next 2 sts on rnd 1, turn.

Next rows: Rep rows 3 and 4 alternately around rnd 1, ending with row 3. Leaving 10-inch end for sewing, fasten off.

Matching sts, sew back lps of last row and starting ch at beg of row 2 tog to form rib. ∎

COWL-NECK SWEATER

DESIGN BY CAROLYN CHRISTMAS AND DARLA HASSELL

INTERMEDIATE

Finished Sizes

Instructions given fit 32–34-inch bust *(small)*; changes for 36–38-inch bust *(medium)*, 40–42-inch bust *(large)* and 44–46-inch bust *(X-large)* are in [ ].

Finished Garment Measurements

Bust: 32½ inches *(small)* [37 inches *(medium)*, 41 inches *(large)*, 44 inches *(X-large)*]

Gauge

11 sc = 3¼ inches; 5 pattern rows = 2 inches
Take time to check gauge.

Pattern Note

Pattern is established in rows 2 and 3.

SWEATER

Back

Row 1: Beg at bottom edge, ch 56 [64, 70, 76], sc in 2nd ch from hook, [ch 1, sk next ch, sc in next ch] across, turn. *(55 [63, 69, 75] sts and ch sps)*
Row 2: Ch 1, sc in first st, sc in next ch-1 sp, [ch 1, sk next st, sc in next ch-1 sp] across to last st, sc in last st, turn.

Materials

- Fine (sport) weight chenille yarn:
  13 [14, 15, 16] oz/1,170 [1,260, 1,350, 1,440] yds/369 [397, 425, 454]g raspberry
- Size I/9/5.5mm crochet hook or size needed to obtain gauge
- Tapestry needle

Row 3: Ch 1, sc in first st, [ch 1, sk next st, sc in next ch-1 sp] across to last 2 sts, ch 1, sk next st, sc in last st, turn.
Next rows: Rep rows 2 and 3 alternately until piece measures 15 [15, 15½, 15½] inches from beg ending with row 3.

Armhole Shaping

Next row: Sl st in first st, sl st in next ch-1 sp, sl st in next st, (sl st, ch 1, sc) in next ch-1 sp, [ch 1, sk next st, sc in next ch-1 sp] across to last 2 sts and last ch sp, leave last 2 sts and last ch sp unworked, turn.
Next 2 rows: Ch 1, sk first st, sc in next ch-1 sp, [ch 1, sk next st, sc in next ch-1 sp] across to last st, leaving last st unworked, turn.
Next rows: Rep rows 2 and 3 alternately until piece measures 19 [19½, 20, 21] inches from beg ending with row 3.

First Shoulder Shaping

Last row: Ch 1, sc in first st, sc in next ch-1 sp, [ch 1, sk next st, sc in next ch-1 sp] 4 times, leaving rem ch sps unworked. Fasten off.

2nd Shoulder Shaping

Last row: Sk across to last 5 ch sps and last 5 sts, join with sc in next ch-1 sp, [ch 1, sk next st, sc in next ch-1 sp] 4 times, sc in last st. Fasten off.

Front

Work same as Back to armholes.

Armhole Shaping

Next row: Sl st in first st, sl st in next ch-1 sp, sl st in

next st, (sl st, ch 1, sc) in next ch-1 sp, [ch 1, sk next st, sc in next ch-1 sp] across to last 2 sts and last ch sp, leave last 2 sts and last ch sp unworked, turn.

Next 3 rows: Ch 1, sk first st, sc in next ch-1 sp, [ch 1, sk next st, sc in next ch-1 sp] across to last st, leaving last st unworked, turn.

Next rows: Rep rows 2 and 3 of Back alternately until length of piece measures 19 [19½, 20, 21] inches from beg ending with row 2.

First Shoulder Shaping

Next row: Ch 1, sc in first st, [ch 1, sk next st, sc in next ch-1 sp] 7 times, leaving rem ch sps unworked, turn.

Next row: Sl st in first st, sl st in next ch-1 sp, sl st in next st, [sc in next ch-1 sp, ch 1, sk next st] 5 times, sc in next ch-1 sp, sc in last st, turn.

Next row: Ch 1, sc in first st, [ch 1, sk next st, sc in next st] 5 times, leaving rem sts unworked, turn.

Next row: Ch 1, sk first st, sc in next ch-1 sp, [ch 1, sk next st, sc in next ch-1 sp] 4 times, sc in last st. Fasten off.

2nd Shoulder

Next row: Sk across to last 7 ch sps and last 8 sts, join with sc in next ch-1 sp, [ch 1, sk next st, sc in next ch-1 sp] 6 times, ch 1, sk next st, sc in last st, turn.

Next row: Ch 1, sc in first st, sc in next ch-1 sp, [ch 1, sk next st, sc in next ch-1 sp] 5 times, leave rem sts and ch sps unworked, turn.

Next row: Ch 1, sk first st, sc in next ch-1 sp, [ch 1, sk next st, sc in next ch-1 sp] 4 times, ch 1, sk next st, sc in last st, turn.

Next row: Ch 1, sc in first st, sc in next ch-1 sp, [ch 1, sk next st, sc in next ch-1 sp] 4 times, leaving last st un-worked. Fasten off.

Sew shoulders seams.

Sew side seams.

Neck Edging

Working on neckline, join with sc in center back ch sp, sc in each ch-1 sp and in end of each row around, with sc in end of each shoulder seam, join with sl st in beg sc. Fasten off.

Armhole Edging

Working in sts and in ends of rows around 1 armhole, join with sc in end of side seam at center bottom, evenly sp 120 sc around armhole, join with sl st in beg sc. Fasten off.

Rep on other armhole.

Bottom Scalloped Edging

Rnd 1: Working in starting ch on opposite side of row 1, join with sc in end of 1 side seam, sc in each ch around with sc in end of other side seam, join with sl st in beg sc.

Rnd 2: Ch 1, sc in first st, sk next st, 5 dc in next st, sk next st, [sc in next st, sk next st, 5 dc in next st, sk next st] around, join with sl st in beg sc. Fasten off.

Cowl Collar

Row 1: Ch 30, sc in 2nd ch from hook, [ch 1, sk next ch, sc in next ch] across, turn. *(29 sts and ch sps)*

Row 2: Ch 1, sc in first st, sc in next ch-1 sp, [ch 1, sk next st, sc in next ch-1 sp] across to last st, sc in last st, turn.

Row 3: Ch 1, sc in first st, [ch 1, sk next st, sc in next ch-1 sp] across to last 2 sts, ch 1, sk next st, sc in last st, turn.

Next rows: Rep rows 2 and 3 alternately until piece fits around Neck Edging, ending with row 3.

At end of last row, fasten off. Matching sts and chs, sew first and last row of piece tog. Sew 1 edge of Cowl Collar to Neck Edging. ■

CLAM SHELL PURSE

DESIGN BY JOYCE BRAGG

INTERMEDIATE

Finished Size

9 x 10 inches, excluding Handle

Materials

- J&P Coats
  Crochet Nylon
  size 18 thread (150 yds
  per tube):
  2 tubes #19 black
- Berroco Crystal FX light
  (light worsted) weight yarn
  (1¾ oz/146 yds/50g per ball):
  1 ball #4701 titanium
- Size G/6/4mm crochet
  hook or size needed to
  obtain gauge
- Tapestry needle
- Sewing needle
- Black thread
- 12 x 24-inch black
  lining material
- 18mm magnetic fastener
- ¼-inch diameter x 10 inches
  long multi temp glue stick
- Stitch marker

Gauge

5 sc = 1 inch

Pattern Note

Weave in loose ends as work progresses.

PURSE

Body

Make 2.

Row 1: With black, ch 14, sc in 2nd ch from hook, sc in each of next 11 chs, 3 sc in last ch, working on opposite side of foundation ch, sc in each of next 12 chs, turn. *(27 sc)*

Row 2: Ch 1, working in **back lp** *(see Stitch Guide)* of each st of Body unless otherwise stated, sc in each of next 12 sts, 3 sc in next st, sc in next st *(center top of Body)*, 3 sc in next st, sc in each of next 12 sts, turn. *(31 sc)*

Row 3: Ch 1, sc in each of next 13 sts, 3 sc in next st, sc in each of next 3 sts, 3 sc in next st, sc in each of next 13 sts, turn. *(35 sc)*

Row 4: Sl st in each of next 3 sts, ch 1, sc in same st as last sl st, *[ch 11, sk next st, sc in next st] 5 times*, sk next st, 3 sc in next st, sc in each of next 5 sts *(center top of Body)*, 3 sc in next st, sk 1 st, sc in next st, rep from * to *, turn.

Row 5: Draw up a lp of titanium, working with both black and titanium, ch 1, *[sk next st, sc in each of next 5 chs, 3 sc in next ch, 5 sc in each of next 5 chs] 5 times*, sk next 2 sc of previous row, with black only, 3 sc in next st, sc in each of next 7 sts *(center top of Body)*, 3 sc in next st, sk next 2 sc of previous row, with both strands, [sc in each of next 5 chs, 3 sc in next ch, sc in each of next 5 chs, sk next st] 5 times, turn.

Row 6: With black only, ch 1, sk first st, *[sc in each of next 5 sts, 3 sc in next st, sc in each of next 5 sts, sk next 2 sts of previous row] 5 times*, 3 sc in next st, sc in each of next 9 sts *(center top of Body)*, 3 sc in next st, sk next 2 sts of previous row, rep between *, turn.

Row 7: Working with both strands, ch 1, sk first st, *[sc in each of next 5 sts, 3 sc in next st, sc in each of next 5 sts, sk next 2 sts of previous row] 5 times*, with black only, 3 sc in next st, sc in each of next 11 sts *(center top of Body)*, 3 sc in next st, sk next 2 sts of previous row, with both strands, rep between *, turn.

Row 8: With black only, ch 1, sk first st, *[sc in each of next 5 sts, 3 sc in next st, sc in each of next 5 sts, sk next 2 sts of previous row] 5 times*, 3 sc in next st, sc in each of next 13 sts *(center top of Body)*, 3 sc in next st, sk next 2 sts of previous row, rep between *, turn.

Rows 9–14: Rep rows 7 and 8, inc 2 sts in each row at center top Body. At the end of row 14 across center top of Body, 3 sc, 25 sc, 3 sc, fasten off first Body section. Do not fasten off black on 2nd Body section.

Handle

Rnd 1: With a separate strand of black, ch 6, sl st in first ch to form a ring, sc in each of next 6 chs, do not join, place stitch marker to mark rnds. *(6 sc)*

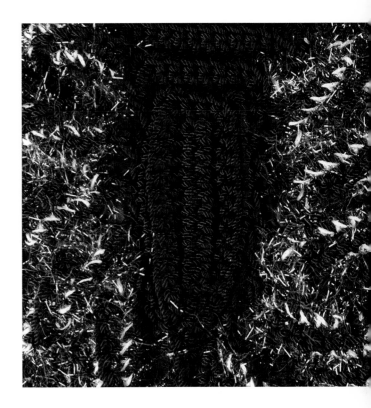

Rnd 2: Sc in each sc around.
Rep rnd 2 until Handle is 10 inches long and glue stick is covered when inserted, sl st in next st, fasten off.

Lining

Using Body as a pattern, cut 2 pieces of black lining material. Leaving top open, sew sides and bottom of seams closed. Allowing ¼-inch seam allowance, attach magnetic fastener at center top of lining. Set lining aside.

Finishing

Pick up Body section that has black still attached, sl st in each of next 4 sts *(placement for end of Handle)*, ch 1, holding WS of Body sections tog and matching sts, sc in each st around to opposite side working 3 sc in each center sc of each 3-sc group to within last 4 sts *(placement for end of Handle)*, fasten off.

Insert lining into Purse, fold raw top edge under and sew to top edge of Purse.

Sew each end of Handle to sk sts at top edge of each Body section. ■

HIDDEN TREASURES SCARF

DESIGN BY BRENDA STRATTON

INTERMEDIATE

Finished Size

5½ x 60 inches

Materials

- Medium (worsted) weight acrylic yarn:
  - 8 oz/400 yds/227g blue
  - 5 oz/250 yds/142g white
- Sizes G/6/4mm and I/9/5.5mm crochet hooks or size needed to obtain gauge
- Sewing needle
- Sewing thread
- Star flower beads:
  - 2 pink pearl
  - 2 green pearl
- White 6mm pearls: 2
- White sewing thread

Gauge

Size I hook: Working in pattern: 2 star sts = 1 inch; 2 star st rows = 1 inch

Special Stitches

Beginning foundation star stitch (beg foundation star st): Yo, insert hook in 2nd ch from hook, yo, pull up lp, yo, insert hook in same ch, yo, pull up lp, sk next ch, insert hook in next ch, yo, pull up lp, yo, pull through all lps on hook, ch 1 to secure *(eye)*.

Foundation star stitch (foundation star st): [Yo, insert hook in same ch as last leg of last star st made, yo, pull up lp] twice, sk next ch, insert hook in next ch, yo, pull up lp, yo, pull through all lps on hook, ch 1 to secure *(eye)*.

Beginning star stitch (beg star st): [Yo, insert hook in eye of last star st made on previous row, yo, pull up lp] twice, insert hook in eye of next star st, yo, pull up lp, yo, pull through all lps on hook, ch 1 to secure *(eye)*.

Star stitch (star st): [Yo, insert hook in same st as last leg of last star st made, yo, pull up lp] twice, insert hook in eye of next star st, yo, pull up lp, yo, pull through all lps on hook, ch 1 to secure *(eye)*.

End star stitch (end star st): [Yo, insert hook in same st as last leg of last star st made, yo, pull up lp] twice, insert hook in ch-1 at end of row, yo, pull up lp, yo, pull through all lps on hook, ch 1 to secure *(eye)*.

Cluster (cl): Holding back last lp of each st on hook, work 2 tr in indicated st, yo, pull through all lps on hook.

SCARF

Foundation row (RS): With size I hook and blue, ch 20, **beg foundation star st** *(see Special Stitches)*, work in **foundation star st** *(see Special Stitches)* across, turn. *(9 star sts)*

Row 1: Ch 1, **beg star st** *(see Special Stitches)*, 7 **star sts** *(see Special Stitches)*, **end star st** *(see Special Stitches)*, turn.

Rows 2–7: Rep row 1 for pattern. At end of last row, fasten off.

With size I hook, working through both thicknesses, join blue with sl st at upper left corner of either Pocket, ch 1, sc in same st, *evenly sp sc across to corner, 3 sc in corner st, evenly sp sc across to next corner, 3 sc in corner, evenly sp sc across to top of same Pocket*, working through Scarf only, evenly sp sc across to top corner of next Pocket, working through both thicknesses, rep between * once, working through Scarf only, evenly sp sc across to first sc, join with sl st in beg sc. **Do not fasten off**.

Edging

Rnd 1: Ch 1, sc in same sc as joining, *ch 2, [sk next sc, sc in next sc, ch 2] across to next corner, (sc, ch 2, sc) in corner sc, rep from * around, join with sl st in beg sc. Fasten off.

Rnd 2: With size I hook and RS facing, join white with sl st in last ch-2 sp before any corner, ch 1, sc in same ch sp, *5 dc in corner ch sp, sc in next ch sp, [3 dc in next ch sp, sc in next ch sp] across to next corner, rep from * around, ending with 3 dc in last ch sp, join with sl st in beg sc. Fasten off.

Flower

Make 2.

With size G hook and white, ch 4, sl st in first ch to form ring, [(ch 4, **cl**—see Special Stitches, ch 4, sl st) in ring] 5 times. Fasten off.

Finishing

Place green star flower bead at center of Flower, then place pink pearl star flower bead on top of the green bead, staggering points. Sew beads in place, starting from the WS of the Flower.

Place 6mm pearl at center of star flowers. Push the needle up through the center of the 2 star flower beads, and through center of pearl, then down through the star flower beads and the Flower in the opposite direction. Rep several times to secure. Fasten off.

Sew 1 Flower to front of each Pocket. ■

Row 8: With size I hook, RS facing, join white with sl st in last eye of last star st worked in previous row, rep row 1.

Rows 9–15: Rep row 1. At end of last row, fasten off.

Row 16: With blue, rep row 8.

Rows 17–23: Rep rows 9–15.

Rows 24–135: [Rep rows 8–23 consecutively] 7 times. At end of last row, fasten off.

Pocket

Make 2.

Foundation row: Rep Foundation row of Scarf.

Rows 1–7: Rep rows 1–7 of Scarf.

Attaching Pockets

Pin Pockets in place at each end of Scarf.

LADYBUG & VICTORIAN BOOT PINS

DESIGNS BY TERRY DAY

EASY

Finished Sizes

Ladybug: 3 inches tall

Victorian boot: 3¼ inches tall

Materials

- Size 10 crochet cotton:

    12 yds peach

    10 yds red

    7 yds black

    1 yd gold metallic

- Size 5/1.90mm steel crochet hook or size needed to obtain gauge
- 1¼-inch pin backs: 2
- 4-inch square black felt
- Stitch markers
- Scrap of fiberfill
- Red fabric paint
- Craft glue
- Hot-glue gun
- Wax paper
- Fabric stiffener
- 4mm pre-strung pearl beads: 11
- 12mm gold ribbon rosette with gold leaves: 1

Gauge

8 sc = 1 inch

Pattern Notes

Weave in loose ends as work progresses.

Do not join rounds unless otherwise stated.

Mark first stitch of each round with stitch marker.

LADYBUG

Body

Rnd 1: With black, ch 5, 2 sc in 2nd ch from hook, sc in each of next 2 chs, 4 sc in last ch, working on opposite side of foundation ch, sc in each of next 2 chs, 2 sc in next ch. *(12 sc)*

Rnd 2: Sc in each sc around.

Rnd 3: Rep rnd 2.

Rnd 4: Sc in next sc, 2 sc in next sc, sc in each of next 3 sc, 2 sc in next sc, sc in next sc, 2 sc in next sc, sc in each of next 3 sc, 2 sc in last sc. *(16 sc)*

Rnd 5: 2 sc in each sc around. *(32 sc)*

Rnd 6: 2 hdc in first sc, hdc in each of next 3 sc, 2 hdc in next sc, sc in each of next 11 sc, 2 hdc in next sc, hdc in each of next 3 sc, 2 hdc in next sc, sc in each of next 11 sc, sl st to join in top of first hdc, fasten off. *(36 sts)*

Head

Rnd 1: With black, ch 2, 6 sc in 2nd ch from hook. *(6 sc)*

Rnd 2: 2 sc in each sc around. *(12 sc)*

Rnd 3: [Sc in next sc, 2 sc in next sc] around, sl st in

next sc, leaving a 6-inch length for sewing, fasten off. *(18 sc)*

Sew Head to end of Body across 6 sts.

Antenna

Make 2.

With 2 strands black, ch 13, leaving a 2-inch length, fasten off. Sew Antenna to center front underside of rnd 3 of Head far enough apart so that when stiffened they can form a heart shape.

Wing

Make 2.

Row 1: With red, ch 3, sc in 2nd ch from hook, sc in next ch, turn. *(2 sc)*

Rows 2–8: Ch 1, 2 sc in first sc, sc in each rem sc across, turn. *(9 sc)*

Rows 9–11: Ch 1, sc in each sc across, turn.

Row 12: Ch 1, **sc dec** *(see Stitch Guide)* in next 2 sc, sc in each sc across to last 2 sc, turn. *(7 sc)*

Row 13: Rep row 12, do not turn. *(5 sc)*

Rnd 14: Ch 1, evenly sp sc in each st around outer edge, sl st to join in beg sc, fasten off.

Finishing

Following manufacturer's directions, stiffen all pieces. Crumple piece of wax paper into a small ball and place underneath Body and each Wing to give rounded dome shape. Using photo as a guide, shape top of Antennas into heart shape, touching at center. Dry completely.

Cut 6 small hearts from black felt, glue 3 to each Wing. Position Head and Body on black felt, trace around outer edge, cut out piece of felt, place fiberfill between Body and felt and glue felt to bottom of Body and Head.

Glue Wings to Body with hot-glue gun.

With red fabric paint, paint red eyes on Head.

To strengthen Antenna, making sure glue does not show on front; place a small bead of glue just where Antenna touch at center back of heart.

Vertically center pin back on back of Ladybug and attach with hot-glue gun.

VICTORIAN BOOT

Toe

Row 1 (RS): With peach, ch 2, sc in 2nd ch from hook, turn. *(1 sc)*

Row 2: Ch 1, 2 sc in first sc, turn. *(2 sc)*

Row 3: Ch 1, 2 sc in first sc, sc in next sc, turn. *(3 sc)*

Row 4: Ch 1, 2 sc in first sc, sc in each rem sc across, turn. *(4 sc)*

Row 5: Ch 1, sc in each of next 3 sc, 2 sc in next sc, turn. *(5 sc)*

Row 6: Rep row 4. *(6 sc)*

Row 7: Ch 1, sc in each sc across, turn.

Row 8: Ch 1, 3 sc in first sc, sc in each rem sc across, turn. *(8 sc)*

Row 9 (RS): Rep row 7, fasten off.

Shaft

Row 1: With peach, ch 8, sc in 2nd ch from hook, sc in each rem ch across, turn. *(7 sc)*

Row 2: Ch 1, sc in each sc across, turn.

Rows 3–11: Rep row 2.

Row 12: Ch 1, 2 sc in first sc, sc in each sc across to last sc, 2 sc in last sc, turn. *(9 sc)*

Row 13: Rep row 12. *(11 sc)*

Rows 14–16: Rep row 2.

Row 17: Rep row 12, fasten off. *(13 sc)*

Row 18: Attach gold metallic with sl st in first sc, ch 1, sc in same sc as beg ch-1, [ch 3, sc in next sc] across, fasten off. *(12 ch-3 sps)*

Sew RS of row 9 of Toe piece to side of Shaft with Toe pointing to left and bottom edges even. With Toe still pointing left, attach peach with sc in side of row 17 of Shaft, sc around outside edge of Boot working 2 sc in very tip of Toe, ending on opposite side of row 17, fasten off.

Heel

Row 1: With top of Shaft facing and Toe pointing to the left, attach peach with sc in first st of Shaft bottom, sc in each of next 3 sts, turn. *(4 sc)*

Row 2: Ch 1, [**sc dec** *(see Stitch Guide)* in next 2 sc] twice, turn. *(2 sc)*

Row 3: Ch 1, 2 sc in first sc, 2 sc in next sc, turn. *(4 sc)*

Row 4: Ch 1, 2 sc in first sc, sc in each of next 2 sc, 2 sc in last sc, fasten off. *(6 sc)*

Sole

Row 1: With Toe facing, attach peach with sc at very tip of Toe, sc in next 5 sc, turn. *(6 sc)*

Row 2: Ch 1, sc in each sc across, turn.

Row 3: Rep row 2, do not turn.

Row 4: Sc in side edge of row 3, sc in each side edge of rows 2 and 1, sl st in next st on bottom of Boot, fasten off.

Finishing

Following manufacturer's directions, stiffen Boot, shape and place on wax paper to dry.

Using photo as a guide, position pearl beads from row 17 to instep of Boot, glue in place with craft glue. Glue ribbon rosette to instep with hot-glue gun. Vertically center pin back on back of Boot and attach with hot-glue gun. ■

LACY PINEAPPLES SHELL

DESIGN BY TAMMY HILDEBRAND

INTERMEDIATE

Finished Sizes

Instructions given fit 32–34-inch bust *(small)*; changes for 36–38-inch bust *(medium)*, 40–42-inch bust *(large)* and 44–46-inch bust *(X-large)* are in [ ].

Finished Garment Measurements

Bust: 36 inches *(small)* [40 inches *(medium)*, 44 inches *(large)*, 48 inches *(X-large)*]

Length: Shoulder to bottom edge of Panels: 13¼ inches *(small)*, 14¼ inches *(medium)*, 15¼ inches *(large)*, 16¼ inches *(X-large)*

Gauge

Size 4 steel hook: Strip = 2¼ inches wide
Size 3 steel hook: Strip = 2½ inches wide
Size 2 steel hook: Strip = 2¾ inches wide
Size 1 steel hook: Strip = 3 inches wide
Size C hook: 22 tr = 4 inches
Size D hook: 20 tr = 4 inches
Size E hook: 18 tr = 4 inches
Size F hook: 16 tr = 4 inches

Materials

- DMC Senso Microfiber light (worsted) weight yarn (1½ oz/150 yds per ball): 9 [11, 13, 15] balls #1101 white **4 MEDIUM**
- Sizes 4/2.00mm, 3/2.10mm, 2/2.20mm and 1/2.25mm steel crochet hooks or sizes needed to obtain gauge
- Sizes C/2/2.75mm, D/3/3.25mm, E/4/3.5mm and F/5/3.75mm crochet hooks or sizes needed to obtain gauge
- Tapestry needle
- Stitch markers

Pattern Notes

Weave in loose ends as work progresses.

Join rounds with a slip stitch unless otherwise stated.

Special Stitch

Shell: 7 dc in indicated st.

SHELL

Strip 1

Row 1: With size 4 [3, 2, 1] steel hook, ch 16, sc in 2nd ch from hook, sc in each of next 6 chs, ch 2, sk next ch, sc in each of next 7 chs, turn. *(14 sc)*

Row 2: Ch 3 *(counts as first dc)*, dc in next st, ch 3, 5 dc in next ch-2 sp, ch 3, sk next 4 sts, dc in each of next 2 sts, turn. *(9 dc)*

Row 3: Ch 3, dc in next st, ch 2, sc in next dc, [ch 3, sc in next dc] 4 times, ch 2, dc in each of next 2 dc, turn. *(4 dc, 5 sc, 4 ch-3 sps)*

Row 4: Ch 3, dc in next st, ch 2, sc in next ch-3 sp, [ch 3, sc in next ch-3 sp] 3 times, ch 2, dc in each of next 2 dc, turn. *(4 dc, 4 sc, 3 ch-3 sps)*

Row 5: Ch 3, dc in next dc, [ch 3, sc in next ch-3 sp] 3 times, ch 3, dc in each of next 2 dc, turn. *(4 dc, 3 sc, 4 ch-3 sps)*

Row 6: Ch 3, dc in next dc, ch 4, sk next ch-3 sp, sc in next ch-3 sp, ch 3, sc in next ch-3 sp, ch 4, sk next ch-3 sp, dc in each of next 2 dc, turn. *(4 dc, 2 sc, 2 ch-4 sps, 1 ch-3 sp)*

Row 7: Ch 3, dc in next dc, ch 5, sc in rem ch-3 sp, ch 5, dc in each of next 2 dc, turn. *(4 dc, 1 sc, 2 ch-5 sps)*

Row 8: Ch 1, sc in each of next 2 dc, sc in each of next 5 chs, ch 2, sk next sc, sc in each of next 5 chs, sc in each of next 2 dc, turn. *(14 sc, ch-2 sp)*

Rows 9–36: [Rep rows 2–8 consecutively] 4 times.

Rows 37–42: Rep rows 2–7. At the end of last rep, fasten off.

Strip 2

Rows 1–42: Rep rows 1–42 of Strip 1.

Strips 3 & 4

Rows 1–36: Rep rows 1–36 of Strip 1.

Rows 37–40: Rep rows 2–5 of Strip 1.

Row 41: Ch 3, dc in next st, [ch 3, sc in next ch-3 sp] twice, fasten off.

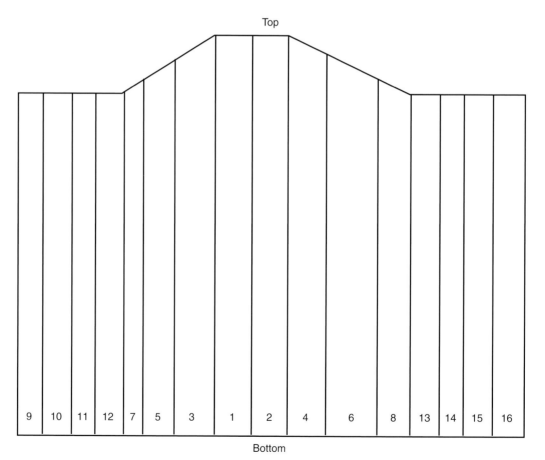

Top

| 9 | 10 | 11 | 12 | 7 | 5 | 3 | 1 | 2 | 4 | 6 | 8 | 13 | 14 | 15 | 16 |

Bottom

Lacy Pineapples Shell Strip Assembly

Strips 5 & 6

Rows 1–36: Rep rows 1–36 of Strip 1.

Rows 37 & 38: Rep rows 2 and 3 of Strip 1.

Row 39: Ch 3, dc in next st, ch 2, sc in next ch-3 sp, ch 3, sc in next ch-3 sp, fasten off.

Strips 7 & 8

Rows 1–36: Rep rows 1–36 of Strip 1.

Row 37: Rep row 2 of Strip 1.

Row 38: Ch 3, dc in next st, ch 2, sc in next st, [ch 3, sc in next st] twice, fasten off.

Strips 9–16

Rows 1–29: Rep rows 1–29 of Strip 1.

Rows 30–35: Rep rows 2–7 of Strip 1. At the end of row 35, fasten off.

Strip Edging

Row 1: Working in ends of rows, join white in side edge of first row with sc, [2 sc in side edge of each dc row, sc in side edge of each sc row] across, fasten off.

Row 2: Working in side edge of rows on opposite side of same Strip, rep row 1.

Strip Assembly

Using diagram as a guide, sew strips tog as indicated.

Strip Bottom Trim

Rnd 1: With size C [D, E, F] hook, working in bottom edge of row 1 of Strips, join white with sc in center of any strip joining, *sk 3 chs of foundation ch, **shell** *(see Special Stitch)* in 4th ch, sk next 3 chs of foundation ch, sc in next ch, sk next 3 chs of foundation ch, shell in next ch, sk next 3 chs of foundation ch, sc in joining of strips, rep from * around, join in beg sc, fasten off.

Strip Top Edging

Rnd 1: With size C [D, E, F] hook, working in sts and chs of last row of Strips, join white with sc in center of Strips 1 and 2 of joining, sc in same sp and work 11 sc evenly spaced across top of same strip *(12 sc)*, work 12 sc evenly spaced across next 6 strips, 13 sc across next strip, 12 sc across each of next 9 strips, join in beg sc. *(194 sc)*

Rnd 2: Ch 3, dc in each st around, join in 3rd ch of beg ch-3, fasten off. *(194 dc)*

Back Panel

Row 1: With size C [D, E, F] hook, ch 100, tr in 5th ch from hook *(first 4 chs count as first tr)*, tr in each rem ch across, turn. *(97 tr)*

Row 2: Ch 3 *(counts as first hdc, ch-1)*, sk next st, hdc in next st, [ch 1, sk next st, hdc in next st] across, turn. *(49 hdc)*

CONTINUED ON PAGE 169

EARTHY GLOW TUNIC VEST

DESIGN BY ZENA LOW

INTERMEDIATE

Finished Sizes

Instructions given fit 32–34-inch bust *(small)*; changes for 36–38-inch bust *(medium)*, 40–42-inch bust *(large)*, 44–46-inch bust *(X-large)*, 48–50-inch bust *(2X-large)* and 52–54-inch bust *(3X-large)* are in [ ].

Finished Garment Measurements

Bust: 36 inches *(small)* [39 inches *(medium)*, 46 inches *(large)*, 49 inches *(X-large)*, 52 inches *(2X-large)*, 56 inches *(3X-large)*]

Gauge

21 sc = 4 inches; 22 rows = 4 inches

Pattern Notes

Weave in loose ends as work progresses.

Join rounds with a slip stitch unless otherwise stated.

For ease in counting beginning foundation chain, attach a safety pin every 50 chains.

Materials

- Patons Brilliant light (light worsted) weight yarn (1¾ oz/166 yds/50g per ball):
  5 [6, 7, 7, 8, 9] balls #03012 earthy glow
- Size H/8/5mm crochet hook or size needed to obtain gauge
- Tapestry needle
- Safety pins

3 LIGHT

VEST

Body

Foundation row (WS): Beg at bottom edge of Vest, ch 188 [206, 242, 260, 278, 296], dc in 4th ch from hook *(first 3 chs count as first dc)*, [ch 2, sk next 2 ch, dc in next ch] across to last ch, dc in last ch, turn. *(64 [70, 82, 88, 94, 100] dc)*

Row 1: Ch 3 *(counts as first dc)*, dc in next dc, ch 2, dc in next dc, [ch 4, tr in each of next 4 dc, dc in next dc, ch 2, dc in next dc] across to last dc, dc in top of turning ch, turn.

Row 2: Ch 3, dc in next dc, ch 2, dc in next dc, [ch 4, sc in each of next 4 tr, ch 4, dc in next dc, ch 2, dc in next dc] across to last dc, dc in top of turning ch, turn.

Row 3: Ch 3, dc in next dc, ch 2, dc in next dc, [ch 4, sc in each of next 4 sc, ch 4, dc in next dc, ch 2, dc in next dc] across to last dc, dc in top of turning ch, turn.

Row 4: Rep row 3.

Row 5: Ch 3, dc in next dc, ch 2, dc in next dc, *ch 2, [tr in next sc, ch 2] 4 times, dc in next dc, ch 2, dc in next dc, rep from * to last dc, dc in top of turning ch, turn.

Row 6: Ch 3, dc in next dc, ch 2, dc in next dc, *[ch 2, dc in next tr] 4 times, [ch 2, dc in next dc] twice, rep from * to last dc, dc in top of turning ch, turn.

Note: Rows 1–6 form pattern and Block pattern.

Rep Block pattern 7 [7, 7, 8, 8, 8] times, ending last rep with a WS row, turn.

Right Front

For Sizes Small, 2X-Large & 3X-Large Only

Row 1: Ch 3, dc in next dc, [ch 2, dc in next dc, ch 4,

tr in each of next 4 dc, ch 4, dc in next dc] 2 [2, 3] times, dc in next ch-2 sp, turn, leaving rem sts unworked.
Row 2: Ch 3, dc in next dc, ch 2, pattern across to end of row, turn.

For Sizes Medium, Large & X-Large Only
Row 1: Ch 3, dc in next dc, [ch 2, dc in next dc, ch 4, tr in each of next 4 dc, ch 4, dc in next dc] twice, [ch 2, dc in next dc] 1 [3, 4] time(s), dc in next ch-2 sp, turn.
Row 2: Ch 3, dc in next dc, ch 2, pattern across to end of row, turn.

For All Sizes
Continue even in pattern until Block pattern has been completed twice, ending with a WS row, fasten off, turn.

Neck Shaping
Row 1: Sk first 8 [8, 9, 10, 11, 11] dc at neckline edge, attach yarn with sl st in next ch-2 sp, ch 3, work in pattern across to end of row, turn.
Row 2: Ch 3, work in pattern across to end of row, turn. Continue in pattern until Block pattern has been completed twice, ending with a WS row, fasten off, turn.

Back
With RS facing, sk next 6 [7, 9, 10, 10, 12] dc, attach yarn with sl st in next ch-2 sp and proceed as follows:

For Sizes Small, Large, & 3X-Large Only
Row 1: Ch 3, [dc in next dc, ch 4, tr in each of next 4 dc, ch 4, dc in next dc, ch 2] 3 [4, 5] times, dc in next dc, ch 4, tr in each of next 4 dc, ch 4, dc in next dc, dc in next ch-2 sp, leaving rem sts unworked, turn.
Row 2: Ch 3, dc in next dc, work in pattern across to last 2 dc, dc in next dc, dc in top of turning ch, turn.

For Sizes Medium, X-Large & 2X-Large Only
Row 1: Ch 3, [dc in next dc, ch 2] 4 [4, 2] times, [dc in next dc, ch 4, tr in each of next 4 dc, ch 4, dc in next dc, ch 2] 3 [4, 5] times, [dc in next dc, ch 2] 3 [3, 1] time(s), dc in next dc, dc in next ch-2 sp, leaving rem sts unworked, turn.

Row 2: Ch 3, [dc in next dc, ch 2] 3 [2, 1] time(s), work in pattern across to last 5 [5, 3] dc, [ch 2, dc in next dc] 4 [4, 2] times, dc in top of turning ch, turn.

For All Sizes
Continue even in pattern until Block pattern has been completed 4 times, ending with a WS row, fasten off, turn.

Left Front
With RS facing, sk next 6 [7, 9, 10, 10, 12] dc, attach yarn with sl st in next ch-2 sp and proceed as follows:

For Sizes Small, 2X-Large & 3X-Large Only
Row 1: Ch 3, [dc in next dc, ch 4, tr in each of next 4 dc, ch 4, dc in next dc, ch 2] 2 [3, 3] times, dc in next dc, dc in top of turning ch, turn.
Row 2: Ch 3, work in pattern across to end of row, turn.

For Sizes Medium, Large & X-Large Only
Row 1: Ch 3, [dc in next dc, ch 2] 1 [3, 4] time(s), [dc in next dc, ch 4, tr in each of next 4 dc, ch 4, dc in next dc, ch 2] twice, dc in next dc, dc in top of turning ch, turn.
Row 2: Ch 3, work in pattern across to end of row, turn.

For All Sizes
Continue even in pattern until Block pattern has been completed twice, ending with a WS row, turn.

Neck Shaping
Row 1: Work in pattern across to last 8 [8, 9, 10, 11, 11] dc, dc in next ch-2 sp at neck edge, leaving rem sts unworked, turn.

Row 2: Ch 3, work in pattern across to end of row, turn. Continue working even in pattern until Block pattern has been completed twice, ending with a WS row, fasten off. Matching sts, sew Fronts to Back across shoulders.

Armhole Edging

Rnd 1: With RS facing, attach yarn with sl st in any st of armhole opening, ch 1, work 60 [60, 80, 80, 80, 80] sc evenly spaced around armhole opening, join in beg sc.
Rnd 2: Ch 1 sc in each sc around, join in beg sc.
Rnd 3: Rep rnd 2, fasten off.
Rep on opposite armhole.

Vest Edging

Rnd 1: With RS facing, attach yarn with sl st in lower Left Front, ch 3, dc in each of next 2 sts, [2 dc in next ch-2 sp, sk next st, 2 dc in next ch-2 sp, dc in next dc] across to last 2 sts, dc in each of next 2 sts, working up Right Front, ch 1, sc evenly spaced up front, working 3 sc at corner points and **sc dec** *(see Stitch Guide)* in next 2 sts at each corner of neck edge, sc in each sc down Left Front, join in top of beg ch-3, do not turn.
Rnd 2: Ch 1, sc in each dc across bottom edge, sc in each sc up Right Front, around neckline and down Left Front, working 3 sc at each point and sc dec in each neckline corner, join in beg sc.
Rnd 3: Ch 1, sc in each sc and in each ch-2 sp and 3 sc in 2nd sc of each corner, 3 sc in 2nd sc of each corner, join in beg sc.
Fasten off and weave in ends.

Ties

Make 4.
Make a ch 15 inches in length, turn ch sideways, sl st in back of 2nd ch from hook, sl st in **back bar** *(see Fig. 1)* of each chain to end of ch, fasten off. Sew first set of Ties to fronts at beg of Neck Shaping and sew 2nd set 4 inches below first set.
Tie each set of Ties in a bow. ■

Back Bar of Chain
Fig. 1

SHORT & SEXY TANK

DESIGN BY MARTY MILLER

INTERMEDIATE

Finished Sizes

Instructions given fit 32–34-inch bust *(small)*; changes for 36–38-inch bust *(medium)*, 40–42-inch bust *(large)* and 44–46-inch bust *(X-large)* are in [ ].

Finished Garment Measurements

Bust: 32 inches *(small)* [36 inches *(medium)*, 40 inches *(large)*, 44 inches *(X-large)*]
Length: 17 inches *(small)* [19 inches *(medium)*, 21 inches *(large)*, 23 inches *(X-large)*]

Gauge

11 sc = 4 inches; 12 sc rows = 4 inches

Pattern Notes

Weave in loose ends as work progresses.
Join rounds with a slip stitch unless otherwise stated.
Top is crocheted vertically with 2 strands held together throughout.

Special Stitch

Foundation single crochet (foundation sc): Ch 2, insert hook in first ch of ch-2, yo, draw up a lp, yo, draw through first lp on hook *(making next foundation chain)*, yo, draw through 2 lps on hook, [insert hook in foundation ch just

Materials

* Tahki Cotton Classic medium (worsted) weight yarn (1¾ oz/108 yds/50g per skein): 7 [9, 11, 13] skeins #3924 dark lavender
* Size K/10½/6.5mm crochet hook or size needed to obtain gauge
* Tapestry needle

made, yo, draw up a lp, yo, draw through first lp on hook *(making the next foundation chain)*, yo, draw through 2 lps on hook] rep indicated number of times.

TANK

Body

Row 1: Work 27 [30, 33, 36] **foundation sc** *(see Special Stitch)* sts, turn. *(27 [30, 33, 36] sc)*

Row 2 (RS): Ch 1, 2 sc in first sc, sc in each of next 11 [14, 14, 17] sc, working in **back lp** *(see Stitch Guide)* of each st, sc in each of next 15 [15, 18, 18] sc *(bottom ribbing)*, turn. *(28 [31, 34, 37] sc)*

Row 3: Ch 1, working in back lps only, sc in each of next 15 [15, 18, 18] sts, sc in each of next 11 [14, 14, 17] sc, 2 sc in next sc, hdc in last sc, turn. *(29 [32, 35, 38] sts)*

Row 4: Ch 1, 2 sc in first st, sc in each of next 13 [16, 16, 19] sts, working in back lp sc in each of each of next 15 [15, 18, 18] sts, turn. *(30 [33, 36, 39] sts)*

Row 5: Ch 1, working in back lps only, sc in each of next 15 [15, 18, 18] sts, sc in each of next 13 [16, 16, 19] sts, 2 sc in next st, hdc in last st, turn. *(31 [34, 37, 40] sts)*

Row 6: Ch 1, 2 sc in first st, sc in each of next 15 [15, 18, 18] sts, sc in back lp of each of next 15 [15, 18, 18] sts, turn. *(32 [35, 38, 41] sts)*

Row 7: Ch 1, working in back lps only, sc in each of next 15 [15, 18, 18] sts, sc in each of next 15 [18, 18, 21] sts, 2 sc in next sc, hdc in last st, turn. *(33 [36, 39, 42] sts)*

Row 8: Ch 1, 2 sc in first st, sc in each of next 17 [20, 20, 23] sts, working in back lps only, sc in each of next 15 [15, 18, 18] sts, turn. *(34 [37, 40, 43] sts)*

For Sizes Medium, Large & X-Large Only

Row 9: Ch 1, working in back lps only, sc in each of next 15 [18, 18] sts, sc in each of next 20 [20, 23] sts, 2 sc in next st, hdc in last st, turn. *([38, 41, 44 sts])*

Row 10: Ch 1, 2 sc in first st, sc in each of next 22 [22, 25] sts, working in back lps only, sc in each of next 15 [18, 18] sts, turn. *([39, 42, 45 sts])*

For Sizes Large & X-Large Only

Row 11: Ch 1, working in back lps only, sc in each of next 18 [18], sc in each of next 22 [25] sc, 2 sc in next sc, hdc in last sc, turn. *([43, 46 sts])*

Row 12: Ch 1, 2 sc in first st, sc in each of next 24 [27] sts, working in back lps only, sc in each of next 18 [18] sts, turn. *([44, 47 sts])*

For Size X-Large Only

Row 13: Ch 1, working in back lps only, sc in each of next 18 sts, sc in each of next 27 sc, 2 sc in next st, hdc in last st, turn. *([48 sts])*

Row 14: Ch 1, 2 sc in first st, sc in each of next 29 sts, working in back lps only, sc in each of next 18 sts, turn. *([49 sts])*

First Strap

For All Sizes

Row 9 [11, 13, 15]: Ch 1, working in back lps only, sc in each of next 15 [15, 18, 18] sts, sc in each of next 19 [24, 26, 31] sts, work 1 foundation sc in same st as last sc, work 13 [13, 13, 13] more foundation sc, turn. *(48 [53, 58, 63] sts)*

Row 10 [12, 14, 16]: Ch 1, sc in each of next 33 [38, 40, 45] sts, working in sc in back lp of each of next 15 [15, 18, 18] sts, turn. *(48 [53, 58, 63] sts)*

Row 11 [13, 15, 17]: Ch 1, working in back lps only, sc in each of next 15 [15, 18, 18] sts, sc in each of next 33 [38, 40, 45] sts, turn. *(48 [53, 58, 63] sts)*

Row 12 [14, 16, 18]: Rep row 10 [12, 14, 16].

Rows 13–16 [15–18, 17–20, 19–22]: [Rep rows 11 and 12 {13 and 14, 15 and 16, 17 and 18}] alternately] twice.

Row 17 [19, 21, 23]: Ch 1, working in back lps only, sc in each of next 15 [15, 18, 18] sts, sc in each of next

23 [28, 30, 35] sts, turn. *(38 [43, 48, 53] sts)*

Row 18 [20, 22, 24]: Ch 1, sc in each of next 22 [27, 29, 34] sts, working in back lps only, sc in each of next 15 [15, 18, 18] sts, turn. *(38 [42, 47, 52] sts)*

Rows 19–30 [21–34, 23–38, 25–42]: [Rep rows 17 and 18 {19 and 20, 21 and 22, 23 and 24} alternately] 6 [7, 8, 9] times.

2nd Strap

Row 31 [35, 39, 43]: Ch 1, working in back lps only, sc in each of next 15 [15, 18, 18] sts, sc in each of next 23 [28, 30, 31] sts, work 1 foundation sc in same st as last sc, work 9 [9, 9, 13] more foundation sc, turn. *(48 [53, 58, 63] sts)*

Rows 32–38 [36–42, 40–46, 44–50]: Rep rows 10–16 [12–18, 14–20, 16–22].

Row 39 [43, 47, 51]: Ch 1, working in back lps only, sc in each of next 15 [15, 18, 18] sts, sc in each of next 18 [23, 25, 30] sts, **sc dec** *(see Stitch Guide)* in next 2 sts, turn. *(34 [39, 44, 49] sts)*

Row 40 [44, 48, 52]: Ch 1, sc dec in next 2 sts, sc in each of next 17 [22, 24, 29] sts, working in back lps only, sc in each of next 15 [15, 18, 18] sts, turn. *(33 [38, 43, 48] sts)*

Row 41 [45, 49, 53]: Ch 1, working in back lps only, sc in each of next 15 [15, 18, 18] sts, sc in each of next 16 [21,

23, 28] sts, sc dec in next 2 sts, turn. *(32 [37, 42, 47] sts)*

Row 42 [46, 50, 54]: Ch 1, sc dec in next 2 sts, sc in each of next 15 [20, 22, 27] sts, working in back lps only, sc in each of next 15 [15, 18, 18] sts, turn. *(31 [36, 41, 46] sts)*

Row 43 [47, 51, 55]: Ch 1, working in back lps only, sc in each of next 15 [15, 18, 18] sts, sc in each of next 14 [19, 21, 26] sts, sc dec in next 2 sts, turn. *(30 [35, 40, 45] sts)*

Row 44 [48, 52, 56]: Ch 1, sc dec in next 2 sts, sc in each of next 13 [18, 20, 25] sts, working in back lps only, sc in each of next 15 [15, 18, 18] sts, turn. *(29 [34, 39, 44] sts)*

Row 45 [49, 53, 57]: Ch 1, working in back lps only, sc in each of next 15 [15, 18, 18] sts, sc in each of next 12 [17, 19, 24] sts, sc dec in next 2 sts, turn. *(28 [33, 38, 43] sts)*

Row 46 [50, 54, 58]: Ch 1, sc dec in next 2 sc, sc in each of next 11 [16, 18, 23] sts, working in back lps only, sc in each of next 15 [15, 18, 18] sts, turn. *(27 [32, 37, 42] sts)*

For Size Small Only

Row 47: Ch 1, working in back lps only, sc in each of next 15 sts, sc in each of next 12 sts, turn. *(27 sts)*

Rows 48–92: Rep rows 2–46. At the end of row 92, turn.

For Sizes Medium, Large & X-Large Only

Row 51 [55, 59]: Ch 1, working in back lps only, sc in each of next 15 [18, 18] sts, sc in each of next 15 [17, 22] sc, sc dec in next 2 sc, turn. *([31, 36, 41] sts)*

Row 52 [56, 60]: Ch 1, sc dec in next 2 sc, sc in each of next 14 [16, 21] sts, working in back lps only sc in each of next [15, 18, 18] sts, turn. *([30, 35, 40] sts)*

Row 53 [57, 61]: Ch 1, working in back lps only, sc in each of next 15 [18, 18] sts, sc in each of next 15 [17, 22] sts, turn. *([30, 35, 40] sts)*

For Size Medium Only

Rows 54–104: Rep rows 2–52. At the end of row 104, turn.

CONTINUED ON PAGE 171

CLASSY CONTINENTAL HAT

DESIGN BY SHIRLEY PATTERSON

EASY

Finished Sizes

Instructions given fit 24¾-inch head circumference; changes for 27-inch head circumference are in [ ].

Gauge

With super bulky yarn: 4 sc = 1½ inches; 3 rows = 1 inch
Take time to check gauge.

Pattern Notes

Work in continuous rounds.

Mark first stitch of each round to keep count of stitches.

Do not join or turn unless otherwise stated.

Materials

- Red Heart Grandé super bulky (super chunky) weight yarn (6 oz/143 yds/170g per skein):
    1 skein #2368 dark brown
- Bernat Soft Bouclé bulky (chunky) weight yarn (5 oz/255 yds/140g per ball):
    1 ball #22927 misty shades
- Size H/8/5mm crochet hook or size needed to obtain gauge
- Stitch markers

HAT

Top

Rnd 1: With dark brown, ch 2, 6 sc in 2nd ch from hook, **do not join or turn** *(see Pattern Note)*. *(6 sc)*

Rnd 2: 2 sc in each st around. *(12 sc)*

Rnd 3: [Sc in next st, 2 sc in next st] around. *(18 sc)*

Rnd 4: [Sc in each of next 2 sts, 2 sc in next st] around. *(24 sc)*

Rnd 5: [Sc in each of next 3 sts, 2 sc in next st] around. *(30 sc)*

Rnd 6: [Sc in each of next 4 sts, 2 sc in next st] around. *(36 sc)*

Rnd 7: [Sc in each of next 5 sts, 2 sc in next st] around. *(42 sc)*

Rnd 8: [Sc in each of next 6 sts, 2 sc in next st] around. *(48 sc)*

Rnd 9: [Sc in each of next 7 sts, 2 sc in next st] around. *(54 sc)*

Rnd 10: [Sc in each of next 8 sts, 2 sc in next st] around. *(60 sc)*

Side

Rnd 11: Working in **back lps** *(see Stitch Guide)*, [sc in each of next 9 sts, 2 sc in next st] around. *(66 sc)*

Rnd 12: Sc in each st around.

Larger Size Only

Rnd 13: [Sc in each of next 10 sts, 2 sc in next st] around. *(72 sc)*

Both Sizes

Rnds 13–22 [14–23]: Sc in each st around. At end of last rnd, join with sl st in next sc.

Brim

Rnd 23 [24]: Ch 3 *(counts as first dc)*, 2 dc in next st, [dc in next st, 2 dc in next st] around, join with sl st in 3rd ch of beg ch-3. *(99 [108] dc)*

Rnd 24 [25]: Ch 3, dc in each st around, join with sl st in 3rd ch of beg ch-3. Fasten off.

Rnd 25 [26]: Join misty shades, with sc in any st, sc in each st around, join with sl st in beg sc. Fasten off.

Finishing

1. Join dark brown with sl st in rem lp on rnd 10 of Top, sl st in each st around, join with sl st in beg sl st. Fasten off.

2. Join misty shades with sl st around any st on rnd 21, sl st around each st around, join with sl st in beg sl st. Fasten off.

3. Rep step 2 on rnd 22 [23]. ■

BEADED MESH SCARF

DESIGN BY BELINDA "BENDY" CARTER

EASY

Finished Sizes

4¼ x 65 inches, excluding

Fringe

Materials

- Medium (worsted) weight yarn:

  3½ oz/175 yds/99g

  light green

- Size H/8/5mm crochet hook or size needed to obtain gauge

- Assorted color of 10mm round opaque beads

- Beading needle

Gauge

15 sts = 4 inches; 6 rows = 3 inches

Special Stitch

Bead single crochet (bead sc): Push bead up to hook, then sc, bead will appear on back side of sts.

SCARF

Row 1 (RS): String 44 beads onto yarn, ch 17, sc in 2nd ch from hook and in each ch across, turn. *(16 sc)*

Row 2: Ch 3 *(counts as first dc)*, dc in next st, [ch 2, sk next 2 sts, **bead sc** *(see Special Stitch)* in next st, ch 2, sk next 2 sts, dc in each of next 2 sts] across, turn.

Row 3: Ch 1, sc in each of first 2 sts, [ch 2, sk next ch sp, dc in next st, ch 2, sk next ch sp, sc in each of next 2 sts] across, turn.

Row 4: Ch 1, sc in each st and ch across, turn. *(16 sc)*

Row 5: Ch 3, dc in next st, [ch 2, sk next 2 sts, sc in next st, ch 2, sk next 2 sts, dc in each of next 2 sts] across, turn.

Row 6: Ch 1, sc in each of first 2 sts, [ch 2, sk next ch sp, dc in next st, ch 2, sk next ch sp, sc in each of next 2 sts] across, turn.

Row 7: Ch 1, sc in each st and ch across, turn. *(16 sc)*

Rows 8–127: [Rep rows 2–7 consecutively] 20 times.

Rows 128–130: Rep rows 2–4. At end of last row, fasten off.

Fringe

Cut 1 strand 5 inches in length, fold strand in half. With WS facing, pull fold through st, pull ends through fold. Pull ends to tighten. Attach Fringe across both short ends of Scarf. Trim ends. ■

BEAD-DAZZLING PURSE

DESIGN BY GLENDA WINKLEMAN

BEGINNER

Finished Size

9½ x 11 inches, excluding
Handles

Gauge

7 sc = 3 inches; 7 sc rows = 3 inches

Materials

- Moda Dea Orbit
  super bulky
  (super chunky)
  weight yarn (1¾
  oz/36 yds/50g per ball):
    3 balls #3934 moonbeam
- Moda Dea Frivolous medium
  (worsted) weight yarn (1¾
  oz/83 yds/50g per ball):
    1 ball #9563 ultra violet
- Size L/11/8mm crochet
  hook or size needed to
  obtain gauge
- Sewing needle and thread
- 1-inch-wide hook-and-loop
  tape: 4 inches
- 1 pair beaded purse handles
  by Handle Connection
- 12 x 19-inch piece of fabric
- Decorative pin

Pattern Notes

Weave in loose ends as work progresses.

Join rounds with a slip stitch unless otherwise stated.

PURSE

Rnd 1: Beg at bottom of Purse, with moonbeam, ch 21, 3 sc in 2nd ch from hook, sc in each rem ch across to last ch, 3 sc in last ch, working on opposite side of foundation ch, sc in each ch across, join in beg sc. *(42 sc)*

Rnd 2: Ch 1, [2 sc in each of next 3 sts, sc in each of next 18 sts] twice, join. *(48 sc)*

Rnds 3–21: Ch 1, sc in each st around, join in beg sc. At the end of rnd 21, fasten off.

Rnd 22: Holding 2 strands of ultra violet tog, join with sc in first st of previous rnd, sc in each st around, join in beg sc, fasten off.

Assembly

With moonbeam, sew handles to center of top edge of Purse.

For lining, with RS tog, fold fabric in half matching 12-inch ends at top edge. Sew ¼-inch seam along each end. Turn top edge down to WS ¼-inch and press. Place lining in Purse and sew in place along top inside edge. Center hook-and-loop tape near top inside of Purse and sew in place. Attach decorative pin to center front of Purse. ■

WRAP-TIE TOP

DESIGN BY MARTY MILLER

INTERMEDIATE

Finished Sizes

Instructions given fit 32–34-inch bust *(small)*; changes for 36–38-inch bust *(medium)*, 40–42-inch bust *(large)* and 44–46-inch bust *(X-large)* are in [ ].

Finished Garment Measurements

Bust: 32 inches *(small)* [36 inches *(medium)*, 41 inches *(large)*, 47½ inches *(X-large)*]

Gauge

5 sts = 2 inches; 6 rows = 2 inches

Pattern Notes

Weave in loose ends as work progresses.

Join rounds with a slip stitch unless otherwise stated.

Top is crocheted with 2 strands held together throughout.

Special Stitch

Foundation single crochet (foundation sc): Ch 2, insert hook in first ch, yo, draw up a lp, yo, draw through first lp on hook to create a ch, yo, draw through 2 lps on hook, [insert hook in the ch created by drawing through first lp on hook, yo, draw up a lp, yo, draw through first lp on hook, yo, draw through both lps on hook] across indicated number of times.

Materials

- Bernat Cool Crochet light (light worsted) weight yarn (1¾ oz/200 yds/50g per ball):
  6 [8, 10, 12] balls #74008 summer cream
- Size K/10½/6.5mm crochet hook or size needed to obtain gauge
- Tapestry needle
- Stitch markers

Pattern Stitch

Row 1: [Sc in next st, dc in next st] across, turn.

Row 2: Ch 2 *(does not count as a stitch)*, [sc in each dc, dc in each sc] across, turn.

TOP

Body

Row 1: Starting at bottom edge, with 2 strands of summer cream held tog, work 113 [129, 145, 161] **foundation sc** *(see Special Stitch)*, turn. *(113 [129, 145, 161] foundation sc)*

Row 2: Ch 2 *(does not count as a st)*, **hdc dec** *(see Stitch Guide)* in next 2 sts, rep row 1 of Pattern Stitch to last 2 sts, hdc dec in last 2 sts, turn. *(111 [127, 143, 159] sts)*

Rows 3–24: Rep row 2. *(67 [83, 99, 115] sts)*

For Size Small Only

Place st marker at beg and end of last row, turn.

For Sizes Medium, Large & X-Large Only

Rows 25–28: Rep row 2 of Body 4 times. *([75, 91, 107] sts)*

For Size Medium Only

Place st marker at beg and end of last row, turn.

For Sizes Large & X-Large Only

Rows 29–32: Rep row 2 of Body 4 times. *([83, 99] sts)*

For Size Large Only

Place st marker at beg and end of last row, turn.

For Size X-Large Only

Rows 33–36: Rep Row 2 of Body 4 times. *([91] sts)* Place st marker at beg and end of last row, turn.

Left Front

Row 25 [29, 33, 37]: Ch 2, hdc dec in next 2 sts, rep row 2 of Pattern Stitch in next 14 [16, 18, 20] sts, turn. *(15 [17, 19, 21] sts)*

Row 26 [30, 34, 38]: Rep row 2 of Pattern Stitch across, ending with sc in last st, turn.

Row 27 [31, 35, 39]: Ch 2, hdc dec in next 2 sts, rep row 2 of Pattern Stitch across, turn. *(14 [16, 18, 20] sts)*

Row 28 [32, 36, 40]: Rep row 2 of Pattern Stitch across, turn.

Row 29 [33, 37, 41]: Ch 2, hdc dec in next 2 sts, rep row 2 of Pattern Stitch across rem sts, turn. *(13 [15, 18, 19] sts)*

Row 30 [34, 38, 42]: Rep row 2 of Pattern Stitch across, turn.

Rows 31–36 [35–40, 39–44, 43–48]: [Rep rows 29 and 30 {33 and 34, 37 and 38, 41 and 42} alternately] 3 times. *(10 [12, 14, 16] sts)*

Rows 37–40 [41–44, 45–48, 49–52]: Rep row 30 [34, 38, 42]. At the end of last rep, fasten off.

Back

Row 25 [29, 33, 37]: Attach yarn in next unworked st after row 24 [28, 32, 36] of Left Front, ch 2, work in Pattern Stitch across 34 [38, 42, 46] sts, sc in next st, turn. *(35 [39, 43, 47] sts)*

Row 26 [30, 34, 38]: Ch 2, dc in first sc, work in Pattern Stitch across, ending with dc in last st, turn.

Rows 27–38 [31–42, 35–46, 39–50]: [Rep rows 25 and 26 {29 and 30, 33 and 34, 37 and 38} alternately] 6 times.

First Shoulder Shaping

Row 39 [43, 47, 51]: Ch 2, work in Pattern Stitch across 10 [12, 14, 16] sts, turn.

Row 40 [44, 48, 52]: Ch 2, work in Pattern Stitch across 10 [12, 14, 16] sts, fasten off.

CONTINUED ON PAGE 172

HOT SUMMER NIGHTS

DESIGN BY COLETTE BLAIR

EXPERIENCED

Finished Sizes

Instructions given fit 32–34-
inch bust *(small)*; changes
for 36–38-inch bust
(medium) and 40–42-inch
bust *(large)* are in [ ].

Finished Garment Measurements

Bust: 32 inches *(small)*
[36 inches *(medium)*,
40 inches *(large)*]

Gauge

4 rows = 1 inch

Pattern Notes

Weave in loose ends as work progresses.
Cut black elastic in half, set aside.

Materials

- J&P Coats Royale Classic size
  10 crochet cotton (350 yds
  per ball):
  - 2 balls #12 black
  - 1 ball #494 victory red
- Size 8/1.50mm steel crochet
  hook or size needed to
  obtain gauge
- Tapestry needle
- Sewing needle and thread
- Size 3 hook and eye
  fasteners: 2
- ¼-inch-wide black elastic:
  30 inches

TOP

Front

Row 1: With black, ch 105 [110, 113], 2 dc in 4th ch
from hook, *sk next 2 chs, (sl st, ch 3, 2 dc) in next ch,
rep from * across, turn. *(35 [37, 39] dc groups)*

Row 2: Ch 2, sl st in ch-3 sp, ch 3, 2 dc in same ch-3 sp,
[sl st in next ch-3 sp, ch 3, 2 dc in same ch-3 sp] across, turn.

Rows 3–9: Rep row 2.

Row 11: Ch 2, sk first sp, [sl st in next ch-3 sp, ch 3, 2 dc in same ch-3 sp] 7 [9, 11] times, turn.

Row 12: Ch 2, sk first sp, [sl st in next ch-3 sp, ch 3, 2 dc in same ch-3 sp] 5 [7, 9] times, sk last sp, turn.

Row 13: Ch 2, sk first sp, sl st in next sp, [sl st in next ch-3 sp, ch 3, 2 dc in same ch-3 sp] 3 [5, 7] times, fasten off, turn.

Row 14: Attach black in row 9 and working across rows 10-13 of Left Front, [ch 4, sl st in next ch-3 sp] across, turn. *(22 [24, 26] ch-4 sps)*

Rows 15–19: [Ch 4, sl st in next ch sp] across, turn.

Row 20: Ch 2, sl st in next ch-4 sp, ch 3, 2 dc in same ch-4 sp, [sl st, ch 3, 2 dc] 21 [23, 25] times, turn. *(22 [24, 26] dc groups)*

Row 21: Sl st in next ch sp, [ch 6, sl st in next ch sp] 13 [14, 16] times, leaving rem lps unworked, turn.

Row 22: Ch 2, sl st in first sp, [ch 6, sl st in next sp] 13 [14, 16] times, turn.

Row 23: Ch 2, sl st in first ch sp, ch 3, 2 dc in same ch sp, [sl st in next ch sp, ch 3, 2 dc in same ch sp] across, fasten off.

Right Front

Row 10: Working from opposite edge of Front, attach black in 4th ch-3 sp, rep row 10 of Left Front.

Rows 11–23: Rep rows 11–23 of Left Front.

Bottom Front

Row 1: With opposite side of row 1 of Front facing, attach black in first st, ch 3, 2 dc in same ch sp, [sk next 2 sts, sl st in next st, ch 3, 2 dc in same st] across, turn.

Row 2: Ch 2, sl st into ch-3 sp, ch 3, 2 dc in same ch-3 sp, [sl st in next ch-3 sp, ch 3, 2 dc in same ch-3 sp] across, turn.

Row 3: Ch 2, sl st into first sp, [ch 6, sl st in next sp] 31 [33, 35] times, turn.

Row 4: Rep row 3.

Row 5: Ch 2, sl st into first ch sp, ch 3, 2 dc in same ch sp, [sl st in next ch sp, ch 3, 2 dc in same ch sp] across, turn. *(31 [33, 35] dc groups)*

Row 6: Ch 2, sk first ch sp, [sl st in next ch sp, ch 3, 2 dc in same ch sp] across to last ch sp, sk last ch sp, turn. *(29 [31, 33] dc groups)*

Left Front

Row 10: Sk first 3 ch-3 sps, sl st in next ch-3 sp, ch 3, 2 dc in same ch-3 sp, [sl st in next ch-3 sp, ch 3, 2 dc in same ch-3 sp] 8 [10, 12] times, turn. *(9 [11, 13] dc groups)*

Rows 7–15: Rep row 6. At the end of last rep, fasten off. *(11 [12, 14] dc groups)*

Row 16: Attach victory red at beg of V-shape angle, [ch 6, sl st in next ch sp] 34 [36, 38] times, turn.

Rows 17 & 18: Ch 2, sc in next ch sp, [ch 6, sl st in next ch sp] across, turn. At the end of row 18, fasten off.

Rows 19–28: Attach black in first victory red ch sp, *ch 3, 2 dc in same ch sp, sl st in next sp*, rep in next 2 victory red sps, ch 2, turn, rep from * to * *(4 ch sps at end of rep)*, ch 2, turn, rep from * to * across 4 ch sps and 2 more victory red ch sps, ch 2, turn, continue toward middle, rep from * to * across ch sps, adding 2 victory ch sps before ch 2, turn. At middle fasten off, rep rows 19-28 on opposite edge.

Rows 29–33: With black, sl st in ch sp, ch 3, 2 dc in same ch sp, [sl st in next ch sp, ch 3, 2 dc in same ch sp] across, turn.

Ruffle

Row 34: [Sl st in ch sp, ch 3, 2 dc in same ch-3 sp, sl st in next ch, ch 3, 2 dc in same ch] in each ch sp across, doubling the dc groups across, turn.

Rows 35–41: Ch 2, [sl st in next ch sp, ch 3, 2 dc in same ch sp] across, turn. At the end of row 41, fasten off.

Back

Make 2.

Row 1: With black, ch 37, 2 dc in 4th ch from hook, [sk 2 chs, sl st in next ch, ch 3, 2 dc in same ch] across, turn. *(12 [12, 12] dc groups)*

Rows 2–24: Ch 2, [sl st into next ch sp, ch 3, 2 dc in same ch sp] across, turn. At the end of row 24 on first back, fasten off. Do not fasten off 2nd piece, turn.

Back Bottom Joining

Row 25: Ch 2, *[sl st in next ch sp, ch 3, 2 dc in same ch sp] across 2nd back section, pick up first back section and rep from * across first section, turn.

Rows 26–33: Ch 2, [sl st in next ch sp, ch 3, 2 dc in same ch sp] across, turn.

Ruffle

Rows 34–41: Rep rows 34–41 of Front Ruffle. Fasten off.

Joining

With RS of Front and Back tog, sew side seams.

Bodice Trim

Row 1: Attach victory red with sl st in first ch sp at back left top, ch 3, 2 dc in same ch sp, [sl st in next ch sp, ch 3, 2 dc in same ch sp] across left back, front and right back, fasten off.

Shoulder Strap

Make 2.

Row 1: With black, ch 133, dc in 4th ch from hook, dc in each rem ch across, turn.

Row 3: Ch 3, dc in each st across, turn.

Row 4: Ch 1, sc in each st across, fasten off.

Row 5: Holding row 4 of shoulder strap to opposite side of foundation ch, place 15-inch length of elastic between layers, attach victory red, and working through both thicknesses, ch 1, sc in each st across, fasten off.

Sew one end of first Strap to center of left side of Back and opposite end of strap to center of left side of Front. Repeat on right side with 2nd Strap. ∎

CITY LIGHTS VEST

DESIGN BY JEWDY LAMBERT

INTERMEDIATE

Finished Sizes

Instructions given fit 40–42-
inch bust *(large)*

Finished Garment Measurement

Bust: 42 inches *(large)*

Materials

- Lion Brand
  Moonlight Mohair
  bulky (chunky) weight yarn
  (1¾ oz/82 yds/50g per ball):
  5 balls #201 rain forest
- Sizes M/13/9mm and
  P/15/10mm crochet hooks
  or sizes needed to
  obtain gauge
- Yarn needle

Gauge

Size M hook: 6 dc = 2½ inches; 3 dc rows = 2½ inches
Size P hook: 3 dc = 1½ inches

Pattern Notes

Weave in loose ends as work progresses.
Join rounds with a slip stitch unless otherwise stated.

VEST

Body

Row 1: With size P hook, ch 100, 2 dc in 3rd ch from hook, *dc in each of next 3 chs, [**dc dec** *(see Stitch Guide)* in next 3 chs] twice, dc in each of next 3 chs**, [3 dc in next ch] twice, rep from * across, ending last rep at **, 3 dc in last ch, turn. *(98 sts)*
Row 2: Ch 3 *(counts as first dc)*, 2 dc in same st as beg ch-3, *dc in each of next 3 dc, [dc dec in next 3 dc] twice, dc in each of next 3 dc**, [3 dc in next dc] twice, rep from * across, ending last rep at **, 3 dc in last dc, turn.
Rows 3–11: Rep row 2.

First Front

Row 12: With size M hook, ch 3, dc in each of next 21 dc, turn. *(22 dc)*

Row 13: Ch 3, dc in each dc across to last dc, leaving last dc unworked, turn. *(21 dc)*

Rows 14–16: Rep row 13. *(18 dc)*

Row 17: Ch 3, dc in each dc across, turn.

Rows 18–21: Rep row 17. At the end of last rep, fasten off.

2nd Front

Row 12: With size M hook, attach yarn in first dc of row 11, ch 3, dc in each of next 21 dc, turn. *(22 dc)*

Rows 13–21: Rep rows 13–21 of First Front.

Back

Row 12: With size M hook, sk next 5 dc of row 11 of Body, attach yarn in next dc, ch 3, dc in each of next 43 dc, leaving rem 5 dc unworked, turn. *(44 dc)*

Row 13: Sl st in next st, ch 3, dc in each dc across to last dc, leaving last dc unworked, turn. *(42 dc)*

Rows 14–19: Ch 3, dc in each dc across, turn.

First Shoulder Shaping

Row 20: With size M hook, ch 3, dc in each of next 17 dc, turn. *(18 dc)*

Row 21: Ch 3, dc in each of next 17 dc, turn.

Row 22: With WS facing, holding Front to Back shoulder, matching sts and working through both thicknesses, sl st in each st across, fasten off.

2nd Shoulder Shaping

Row 20: With size M hook, sk next 6 dc of row 19 for back neck opening, attach yarn in next dc, ch 3, dc in each of next 17 dc, turn.

Rows 21 & 22: Rep rows 21 and 22 of First Shoulder Shaping.

Trim

Rnd 1: With size M hook, attach yarn at shoulder seam, ch 1, sc in each sc evenly spaced around outer edge of Vest, join in beg sc, fasten off.

Armhole Trim

Rnd 1: With size M hook, attach yarn at underarm, ch 1, sc evenly spaced around armhole opening, join in beg sc, fasten off.

Rep on opposite armhole opening. ■

SUEDE FRINGED VEST

DESIGN BY TAMMY HILDEBRAND

INTERMEDIATE

Finished Sizes

Instructions given fit 32–34-inch bust *(small)*; changes for 36–38-inch bust *(medium)*, 40–42-inch bust *(large)* and 44–46-inch bust *(X-large)* are in [ ].

Finished Garment Measurement

Bust: 35 inches *(small)* [39 inches *(medium)*, 43 inches *(large)*, 47 inches *(X-large)*]

Gauge

9 sc = 4 inches; 8 rows = 4 inches

Pattern Notes

Weave in loose ends as work progresses.
Join rounds with a slip stitch unless otherwise stated.

VEST

Front Panel

Make 2.
Row 1: Ch 14 [16, 18, 20], sc in 2nd ch from hook, sc in each rem ch across, turn. *(13 [15, 17, 19] sc)*
Row 2: Ch 1, sc in each st across, turn.
Row 3: Ch 1, 2 sc in first st, sc in each rem st across, turn. *(14 [16, 18, 20] sc)*

Materials

* Lion Brand Lion Suede bulky (chunky) weight yarn (3 oz/122 yds/85g per skein): 3 [4, 4, 5] skeins #126 coffee
* Size J/10/6mm crochet hook or size needed to obtain gauge
* Tapestry needle
* 12 [14, 16, 18] wooden pony beads

5 BULKY

Rows 4–9: [Rep rows 2 and 3 alternately] 3 times. *(17 [19, 21, 23] sc at end of last row)*
Rows 10–21: Rep row 2.
Row 22: Ch 1, sc in first st, sc in each st to last st, leaving last st unworked, turn. *(16 [18, 20, 22] sc)*
Row 23: Rep row 2.
Rows 24–29: [Rep rows 22 and 23 alternately] 3 times. *(13 [15, 17, 19] sc)*
Row 30: Sl st in next st, ch 1, sc in same st, sc in each st up to last st, leaving last st unworked, turn. *(11 [13, 15, 17] sc)*
Row 31: Rep row 2.
Rows 32–35 [32–37, 32–39, 32–41]: [Rep rows 30 and 31 alternately] twice [3, 4, 5] times. *(7 [9, 11, 13] sc)*
Rows 36–44 [38–46, 40–48, 42–50]: Rep row 2. At the end of last rep, fasten off.

Back Panel

Row 1: Ch 41 [46, 51, 56], sc in 2nd ch from hook, sc in each rem ch across, turn. *(40 [45, 50, 55] sc)*
Row 2: Ch 1, sc in each st across, turn.
Rows 3–29: Rep row 2.
Row 30: Sl st in next st, ch 1, sc in same st, sc in each st across to last st, leaving last st unworked, turn. *(38 [43, 48, 53] sc)*
Row 31: Rep row 2.
Rows 32–35: [Rep rows 30 and 31 alternately] twice. *(34 [39, 44, 49] sc)*
Rows 36–41 [36–43, 36–45, 36–47]: Rep row 2.

First Shoulder

Row 42 [44, 46, 48]: Ch 1, sc in first st, sc in each of next 5 [7, 9, 11] sts, leaving rem sts unworked, turn. *(6 [8, 10, 12] sc)*

14 [16, 18, 20] rows open for armhole. Sew side seam on opposite edge.

Edging

Rnd 1: Working in row ends, join with sc in first row of right Front Panel, sc in each row, working in sts across Back, sc in each of next 1 [2, 2, 2] sts, [{**sc dec** *(see Stitch Guide)* in next 2 sts} twice, sc in each of next 4 sts, {sc dec in next 2 sts} twice] twice, sc in each of next 1 [3, 2, 3] sts, working in row ends of left Front Panel, sc in each row, working in opposite side of foundation ch of row 1, sc in each ch, join in beg sc. *(170 [185, 198, 212] sc)*

Front Trim

Row 1: Ch 2, hdc in each of next 43 [45, 47, 49] sts, sc in each of next 1 [2, 2, 3] sts, [sc dec in next 2 sts] twice, [sc in each of next 2 sts, sc dec in next 2 sts] twice, sc dec in next 2 sts, sc in each of next 1 [2, 2, 2] sts, hdc in each rem st down front, fasten off. *(11 [13, 13, 14] sc, 88 [92, 96, 100] hdc)*

Armhole Edging

Rnd 1: Working in row ends around armhole opening, join with sc in any row, sc in each row around, join in beg sc, fasten off. *(28 [32, 36, 40] sc)*
Rep on opposite armhole opening.

Bottom Fringe

Cut 66 [75, 84, 93] yarn lengths each 18 inches long. Fold 1 strand in half, working in sc across bottom, insert hook in st, draw strand through at fold to form a lp on hook, draw cut strands through lp on hook, pull to tighten ends. Trim ends even.

Bead Fringe

Cut 12 [14, 16, 18] yarn lengths each 11 inches long. Place 1 bead on each strand, with bead at center, fold strand in half. With front facing, working around post of sts of row 21 on right Front Panel, [insert hook around post of next st, draw fold through to form a lp, pushing bead close to front of Vest, draw cut ends through lp on hook, tighten, sk next st] 6 [7, 8, 9] times. Rep Bead Fringe on opposite Front Panel. ■

Rows 43 & 44 [45 & 46, 47 & 48, 49 & 50]: Rep row 2. At the end of last rep, fasten off.

2nd Shoulder

Row 42 [44, 46, 48]: Sk next 22 [23, 24, 25] sts on row 41 [43, 45, 47], attach yarn with sc in next st, sc in each of next 5 [7, 9, 11] sts, turn. *(6 [8, 10, 12] sc)*
Rows 43 & 44 [45 & 46, 47 & 48, 49 & 50]: Rep row 2. At the end of last rep, fasten off.

Assembly

Matching sts on last row of Back Panel with sts on last row of Front Panel, sew shoulder seam tog. Rep for 2nd Front Panel.
Starting at row 1, matching row ends of rows 1–30 of Front and Back Panels, sew side seam tog, leaving last

GLAM GAL HAT & PURSE

DESIGNS BY SUE CHILDRESS

INTERMEDIATE

Finished Sizes

Hat: 22 inches in diameter

Purse: 6-inch base x 7 inches
    high, excluding Drawstrings

Materials

- Araucania Nature
  Wool medium
  (worsted) weight
  yarn (3½ oz/240
  yds/100g per skein):
      1 skein #RO17 *pink* (A)
      2 skeins #RO29 *shaded
          pinks variegated* (B)
- Sirdar Boa bulky (chunky)
  weight yarn (1¾ oz/102
  yds/50g per skein):
      1 skein #024 damask
          rose (C)
- Tahki Flower bulky (chunky)
  weight yarn (1 oz/38 yds/
  25g per skein):
      1 skein #16 azalea (D)
- Sizes G/6/4mm and
  K/10½/6.5mm crochet
  hooks or sizes needed to
  obtain gauge
- Tapestry needle
- Stitch marker
- 2½-inch square cardboard

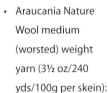

Gauge

Size G hook: 5 sc = 1 inch; 5 sc rnds = 1 inch

Size K hook: 3 hdc = 1 inch; 3 hdc rnds = 1½ inches

Pattern Notes

Weave in loose ends as work progresses.
Join rounds with a slip stitch unless otherwise stated.

HAT

Rnd 1: With size G hook and B, ch 4, join in first ch to form a ring, ch 1, 6 sc in ring, do not join rnds, use st marker to mark rnds. *(6 sc)*
Rnd 2: 2 sc in each sc around. *(12 sc)*
Rnd 3: [2 sc in next sc, sc in next sc] around. *(18 sc)*
Rnd 4: [2 sc in next sc, sc in each of next 2 sc] around. *(24 sc)*
Rnd 5: [2 sc in next sc, sc in each of next 3 sc] around. *(30 sc)*
Rnd 6: [2 sc in next sc, sc in each of next 4 sc] around. *(36 sc)*

Rnd 7: [2 sc in next sc, sc in each of next 5 sc] around. *(42 sc)*
Rnd 8: [2 sc in next sc, sc in each of next 6 sc] around. *(48 sc)*
Rnd 9: [2 sc in next sc, sc in each of next 7 sc] around. *(54 sc)*
Rnd 10: [2 sc in next sc, sc in each of next 8 s] around. *(60 sc)*
Rnd 11: [2 sc in next sc, sc in each of next 9 sc] around. *(66 sc)*
Rnd 12: [2 sc in next sc, sc in each of next 10 sc] around. *(72 sc)*
Rnd 13: [2 sc in next sc, sc in each of next 11 sc] around. *(78 sc)*
Rnd 14: [2 sc in next sc, sc in each of next 12 sc] around. *(84 sc)*
Rnd 15: [2 sc in next sc, sc in each of next 13 sc] around. *(90 sc)*
Rnd 16: Ch 2 *(counts as first hdc)*, **bphdc** *(see Stitch Guide)* around each sc around, join in 2nd ch of beg ch-2. *(90 hdc)*
Rnd 17: Ch 2, hdc in each st around, join in 2nd ch of beg ch-2.
Rnds 18–20: Rep rnd 17. Turn at the end of rnd 20.
Rnd 21 (WS): Drop B, draw up a lp of D, sc in each st around, join in beg sc.
Rnd 22: Ch 1, sc in each st around, join in beg sc, fasten off, turn.
Rnd 23 (RS): Draw up a lp of B, ch 2, hdc in each st around, join in 2nd ch of beg ch-2. *(90 hdc)*
Rnds 24–27: Rep rnd 17. At the end of rnd 27, fasten off.
Rnd 28: With size K hook, attach 2 strands of C in any hdc, ch 2, hdc in each hdc around, join in 2nd ch of beg ch-2, fasten off.

PURSE

Body

Rnd 1: With size K hook and 2 strands of B, leaving 2-inch length at beg, ch 3, 8 hdc in first ch of ch-3, join in 3rd ch of beg ch-3. Draw end of beg tail to close opening, knot ends to secure. *(9 hdc)*

Rnd 2: Ch 2 *(counts as first hdc)*, hdc in same st as beg ch-2, 2 hdc in each rem hdc around, join in 2nd ch of beg ch-2. *(18 hdc)*

Rnd 3: Ch 2, hdc in next hdc, [2 hdc in next hdc, hdc in next hdc] around, join in 2nd ch of beg ch-2. *(26 hdc)*

Rnd 4: Rep rnd 3. *(38 hdc)*

Rnd 5: Ch 2, hdc in same st as beg ch-2, hdc in next hdc, [2 hdc in next hdc, hdc in each of next 2 hdc] 11 times, 2 hdc in next hdc, hdc in next hdc, 2 hdc in next hdc, join in 2nd ch of beg ch-2. *(52 hdc)*

Rnd 6: Ch 2, [hdc in each of next 2 hdc, 2 hdc in next hdc] 16 times, hdc in each of next 3 hdc, join in 2nd ch of beg ch-2. *(68 hdc)*

Rnd 7: Ch 2, bphdc around each hdc around, join in top of beg ch-2.

Rnd 8: Ch 2, hdc in each st around, join in 2nd ch of beg ch-2.

Rnds 9–14: Rep rnd 8. **Turn** at the end of rnd 14.

Rnd 15 (WS): Draw up a lp of D, ch 2, hdc in each hdc around, join in 2nd ch of beg ch-2.

Rnd 16: Ch 2, hdc in each hdc around, join in 2nd ch of beg ch-2, fasten off, turn.

Rnd 17 (RS): Attach 2 strands of A in any hdc, ch 2, hdc in each hdc around, join in 2nd ch of beg ch-2.

Rnds 18–21: Rep rnd 8. At the end of rnd 21, fasten off.

Rnd 22: Attach 2 strands of C in any hdc, ch 2, hdc in each hdc around, join in 2nd ch of beg ch-2, fasten off.

Drawstring

Make 2.

With size K hook and 2 strands of A, ch 100, fasten off. Weave each Drawstring through rnd 19 in opposite directions. Knot first Drawstring ends tog approximately 2 inches from end, rep at opposite edge.

Tassel

Make 4.

Holding 2 strands of A and 1 strand of D tog, wrap 15 times around cardboard. With a 6-inch length of A, pass through top edge and knot, remove from cardboard, tie another length of A approximately 1 inch down from top of Tassel, trim bottom edge of strands evenly. Attach 1 Tassel to each end of Drawstring. ∎

CANYON COLORS HAT & SCARF

DESIGNS BY ALINE SUPLINSKAS

BEGINNER

Finished Sizes

Scarf: 5½ x 64 inches

Hat: 22 inches in circumference

Gauge

Scarf: (Ch 1, sc) = 1 inch; 3 rows = 1 inch

Hat: 5 dc = 2 inches; 3 rows = 1¾ inches

Pattern Notes

Weave in loose ends as work progresses.

Join rounds with a slip stitch unless otherwise stated.

Materials

5 BULKY

- Lion Brand Color Waves bulky (chunky) weight yarn (3 oz/125 yds/85g per skein):
    2 skeins #398 pebble beach
- Lion Brand Fun Fur bulky (chunky) weight yarn (1¾ oz/60 yds/50g per ball):
    2 balls #124 champagne
- Size K/10½/6.5mm crochet hook or size needed to obtain gauge
- Tapestry needle
- Elastic thread: 3 yds
- Stitch marker

SCARF

Row 1: With pebble beach, ch 183 loosely, sc in 3rd ch from hook, [ch 1, sk 1 ch, sc in next ch] across, turn. *(91 ch-1 sps)*

Row 2: Ch 2 *(counts as a ch sp)*, sc in first sp, [ch 1, sc in next ch sp] across, turn.

Rows 3–16: Rep row 2. At the end of row 16, fasten off.

HAT

Rnd 1 (RS): With pebble beach, ch 3, sl st in first ch to form a ring, ch 3 *(counts as first dc)*, 13 dc in ring, join in 3rd ch of beg ch-3. *(14 dc)*

Rnd 2: Working in sps between sts, sl st in next sp, ch 3, dc in same sp, 2 dc in each rem sp around, join in 3rd ch of beg ch-3. *(28 dc)*

Rnd 3: Sl st in sp between dc sts, ch 3, [dc in next sp between dc sts] around, join in 3rd ch of beg ch-3.

Rnd 4: Ch 3, [dc in each of next 3 dc, 2 dc in next dc] 6 times, dc in each of next 3 dc, join in 3rd ch of beg ch-3. *(34 dc)*

Rnd 5: Ch 3, [dc in each of next 4 dc, 2 dc in next dc] 6 times, dc in each of next 3 dc, join in 3rd ch of beg ch-3. *(40 dc)*

Rnd 6: Ch 3, [dc in each of next 5 dc, 2 dc in next dc] 6 times, dc in each of next 3 dc, join in 3rd ch of beg ch-3. *(46 dc)*

CONTINUED ON PAGE 173

FLOWER PURSE

DESIGNS BY JULENE WATSON

EASY

Finished Size

3¼ x 3¾ inches, excluding
Neck Loop

Materials

2 FINE

- Fine (sport) weight yarn:
  ½ oz/50 yds/14g each white, pink and green
- Size E/4/3.5mm crochet hook or size needed to obtain gauge
- Tapestry needle
- Stitch marker
- ½-inch pearl shank button

Gauge

Rose = 3 inches in diameter; [sc, ch 1] 4 times = 1 inch

Pattern Notes

Weave in loose ends as work progresses.

Join rounds with a slip stitch unless otherwise stated.

This design can be made larger using light or medium weight yarn or smaller by using size 10 crochet cotton.

Special Stitches

3-treble crochet cluster (3-tr cl): *Yo hook twice, insert hook in indicated st, yo, draw up lp, [yo, draw through 2 lps on hook] twice, rep from * twice, yo, draw through all 4 lps on hook.

Beginning 3-treble crochet cluster (beg 3-tr cl): Ch 3 *(counts as first tr)*, *yo hook twice, insert hook in indicated st, yo, draw up lp, [yo, draw through 2 lps on hook] twice, rep from * once, yo, draw through all 3 lps on hook.

PURSE

Purse Front

Rnd 1: With white, ch 4, join in first ch to form a ring, **beg 3-tr cl** *(see Special Stitches)* in ring, ch 2, (**3-tr cl**—*see Special Stitches*, ch 2) 5 times in ring, join in top of beg 3-tr cl. *(6 tr cls, 6 ch-2 sps)*

Rnd 2: Sl st into ch-2 sp, (beg 3-tr cl, ch 2, 3-tr cl, ch 2) in same ch-2 sp, (3-tr cl, ch 2) twice in each ch-2 sp around, join in top of beg 3-tr cl. *(12 tr cls, 12 ch-2 sps)*

Rnd 3: Rep rnd 2. At the end of rnd 2, fasten off. *(24 tr cls, 24 ch-2 sps)*

Purse Back

Rnds 1–3: Rep rnds 1–3 of Purse Front. At the end of rnd 3, do not fasten off.

Row 4: Now working in rows, sl st in next ch-2 sp, beg 3-tr cl in same ch-2 sp, [ch 1, 3-tr cl in next ch-2 sp] 5 times, leaving a 6-inch length of yarn, fasten off. *(6 tr cl, 5 ch-2 sps)*

Leaf

Row 1: With green, ch 15, sc in 2nd ch from hook, sc in each rem ch across to last ch, 5 sc in last ch *(tip of leaf)*, working on opposite side of foundation ch, sc in each ch across, 3 sc in last ch *(bottom tip)*.

Row 2: Ch 1, working in **back lp** *(see Stitch Guide)* of each st, sc in each st ending 4 sc from the center sc of tip, turn.

Row 3: Ch 1, working in **front lp** *(see Stitch Guide)* of each st, sc in each st down side with 3 sc in center sc at bottom tip, then sc up other side, ending 3 sc from tip of leaf, turn.

Row 4: Ch 1, working in back lp of each st, sc in each st down side with 3 sc in center sc at bottom tip, then sc up other side, ending 3 sc from tip of leaf, turn.

Row 5: Rep row 3, fasten off.

Carefully sew the Leaf across Purse Front with bottom tip near center of the Purse Front and tip of Leaf slightly out over the edge of the Purse Front.

Rose

Rnd 1: With pink, ch 6, join in first ch to form a ring, ch 1, [sc in ring, ch 3] 6 times, join in beg sc. *(6 ch-3 sps)*

Rnd 2: Ch 1, (sc, hdc, 3 dc, hdc, sc) in each ch-3 sp around, join in beg sc. *(6 petals)*

Rnd 3: Working behind petals, sl st around **back post** *(see Stitch Guide)* of sc post of rnd 1, ch 5, [sl st around post of next sc of rnd 1, ch 5] 5 times, join in beg sl st. *(6 ch-5 sps)*

Rnd 4: Ch 1, (sc, hdc, 5 dc, hdc, sc) in each ch-5 sp around, join in beg sc. *(6 petals)*

Rnd 5: Working behind petals, sl st around sl st of rnd 3, ch 7, [sl st around next sl st of rnd 3, ch 7] 5 times, join in beg sl st. *(6 ch-7 sps)*

Rnd 6: Ch 1, (sc, hdc, 7 dc, hdc, sc) in each ch-7 sp around, join in beg sc. *(6 petals)*

Rnd 7: Working behind petals, sl st around sl st of rnd 5, ch 9 [sl st around next sl st of rnd 5, ch 9] 5 times, join in beg sl st. *(6 ch-9 sps)*

Rnd 8: Ch 1, (sc, hdc, 9 dc, hdc, sc) in each ch-9 sp around, join in beg sc, fasten off. *(6 petals)*

Finishing

Rnd 1: With WS of Purse Front and Back tog, with Front facing, matching tr cl sts and working through both thicknesses, attach white with sl st in center bottom cl, ch 1, sc in same tr cl, [2 sc in next ch-2 sp, sc in next tr cl] 8 times, ch 150 *(Neck Loop)*, sk the next 6 tr cl of row 4 of Purse Back, sk next tr cl, working through both thicknesses, [sc in next tr cl, 2 sc in next ch-2 sp] around to beg of rnd, join in beg sc, fasten off.

With rem length of white yarn, position the Rose so that 2 outer petals of Rose are centered across the 6 tr cl of row 4 of purse back, sew petals to tr cl and ch-2 sps across row 4.

Position pearl shank button on front at center of Rose, sew button to Purse Front. To close Purse, pass button through center of Rose. ■

SEASIDE SCALLOPS REVERSIBLE BAG

DESIGN BY JEWDY LAMBERT

INTERMEDIATE

Finished Size

12 x 13 inches, excluding
Shoulder Strap

Gauge

5 dc = ¾ inch; 3 dc rows = ¾ inch

Pattern Note

Weave in loose ends as work progresses.

Materials

- Fine (sport) weight cotton
  yarn (1¾ oz/166 yds/50g
  per ball):
    3 balls light sage
- Size C/2/2.75mm crochet
  hook or size needed to
  obtain gauge
- Tapestry needle
- Stitch markers

BAG

Body

Row 1: Ch 207, dc in 6th ch from hook, sk next 2 chs, 5 dc in next ch, sk next 2 chs, dc in next ch, place marker *(side panel)*, sc in next ch, *ch 3, sk next 2 chs, sc in next ch, [ch 5, sk next 3 chs, sc in next ch] 3 times, ch 3, sk next 2 chs, sc in next ch*, rep between * 4 times, place marker *(front panel)*, dc in next ch, ch 1, sk next ch, dc in next ch, sk next 2 chs, 5 dc in next ch, sk next 2 chs, dc in next ch, ch 1, sk next ch, dc in next ch, place marker *(side panel)*, sc in next ch, rep between * 5 times *(back panel)*, turn.

Row 2: Ch 4 *(counts as first dc, ch-1)*, dc in next dc, sk next 2 dc of 5-dc group, 5 dc in next dc, sk next 2 dc of same 5-dc group, dc in next dc, ch 1, dc in next dc, place marker, dc in next st, *ch 3, sk next ch-3 sp, sc in next ch sp, 9 dc in next ch sp, sc in next ch sp, ch 3, sk next ch-3 sp**, 3 dc in next sc*, rep between * 4 times, ending last rep at **, dc in next sc, place marker, dc in next dc, ch 1, dc in next dc, sk next 2 dc of 5-dc group, 5 dc in next dc, sk next 2 dc of same 5-dc group, dc in next dc, ch 1, dc in next dc, place marker, rep between * 5 times, turn.

Row 3: Ch 4, dc in next dc, sk next 2 dc of 5-dc group, 5 dc in next dc, sk next 2 dc of same 5-dc group, dc in next dc, ch 1, dc in next dc, place marker, sc in next st, *ch 1, sk next 3 chs and next sc, dc in next dc, [ch 1, dc in next dc] 8 times, ch 1, sk next sc and next ch-3 sp**, sc in each of next 3 sts*, rep between * 4 times, ending last rep at **, sc in next st, place marker, dc in next dc, ch 1, dc in next dc, sk next 2 dc of 5-dc group, 5 dc in next dc, sk next 2 dc of same 5-dc group, dc in next dc, ch 1, dc in next dc, place marker, rep between * 5 times, turn.

Row 4: Ch 4, dc in next dc, sk next 2 dc of 5-dc group, 5 dc in next dc, sk next 2 dc of same 5-dc group, dc in next dc, ch 1, dc in next dc, place marker, dc in next dc, [ch 1, sk next ch-1 sp, dc in next dc] 3 times, ch 1, sk next ch-1 sp, (dc, ch 1, dc) in next dc, ch 1, sk next ch-1 sp, dc in next dc] 4 times *(dc-crescent completed)*, sk next ch-1 sp and next sc, sc in next sc**, sk next sc and next ch-1 sp*, rep from * 4 times, ending last rep at **, place marker, dc in next dc, ch 1, dc in next dc, sk next

group, 5 dc in next dc, sk next 2 dc of same 5-dc group, dc in next dc, ch 1, dc in next dc *(side panel)*, sc in each st across main Body of Bag**, dc in next dc, rep from *, ending last rep at **, turn.

Row 42: *Ch 4, dc in next dc, sk next 2 dc of 5-dc group, 5 dc in next dc, sk next 2 dc of same 5-dc group, dc in next dc, ch 4, sc in next dc, sc in each sc across Body of Bag**, sc in next dc, rep from * across, ending last rep at **, fasten off.

First Shoulder Strap

Row 1: Attach light sage in 3rd ch of ch-4 of side panel, ch 4, dc in next dc, sk next 2 dc of 5-dc group, 5 dc in next dc, sk next 2 dc of same 5-dc group, dc in next dc, ch 1, dc in next dc, turn.

Row 2: Ch 4, dc in next dc, sk next 2 dc of 5-dc group, 5 dc in next dc, sk next 2 dc of same 5-dc group, dc in next dc, ch 1, dc in next dc, turn.

Rows 3–40: Rep row 2. At the end of last rep, fasten off.

2nd Shoulder Strap

Rows 1–39: Rep rows 1–39 of First Shoulder Strap.

Row 40: Rep row 2 of First Shoulder Strap, do not turn, using care that straps are not twisted, matching sts and working through both thicknesses, sl st across, fasten off.

Bottom

Row 1: Ch 12, dc in 4th ch from hook, dc in each of next 8 chs, turn. *(10 dc)*

Row 2: Ch 3 *(counts as first dc)*, dc in each dc across, turn. *(10 dc)*

Rows 3–35: Rep row 2. At the end of row 35, fasten off.

Edging

Row 1: Working down side edge of Bag, attach light sage in side edge of last row of Body, working in first dc of side panel, ch 1, sc evenly sp to bottom edge, working in foundation ch and side edge of Bottom, sc evenly spaced across, working up opposite side edge, sc evenly spaced in dc of side panel to top edge of Body, fasten off.

Rep row 1 of Edging on opposite side edge of Body. ∎

2 dc of 5-dc group, 5 dc in next dc, sk next 2 dc of same 5-dc group, dc in next dc, ch 1, dc in next dc, place marker, rep between * 5 times, turn.

Row 5: Ch 4, dc in next dc, sk next 2 dc of 5-dc group, 5 dc in next dc, sk next 2 dc of same 5-dc group, dc in next dc, ch 1, dc in next dc, place marker, dc in next st, ch 3, *sc in 3rd dc of dc-crescent, ch 5, sk next ch-1 sp, sk next dc, sc in next ch, ch 5, sk next dc, ch-1 sp and next dc, sc in next ch-1 sp, ch 5, sk next dc and next ch-1 sp, sc in next dc, ch 3, sk rem sts of dc-crescent, 1 dc in next st**, ch 3*, rep between * 4 times, ending last rep at **, place marker, dc in next dc, ch 1, dc in next dc, sk next 2 dc of 5-dc group, 5 dc in next dc, sk next 2 dc of same 5-dc group, dc in next dc, ch 1, dc in next dc, place marker, rep between * 5 times, turn.

Row 6–37: [Rep rows 2–5 consecutively] 8 times.

Rows 38–40: Rep rows 2–4.

Row 41: Ch 4, *dc in next dc, sk next 2 dc of 5-dc

FASHION FLOWER PINS

DESIGNS BY DARLA SIMS

RAINBOW BRIGHT

 EASY

Finished Size
3½ inches in diameter

Materials

- Lion Brand Incredible Ribbon bulky (chunky) weight yarn (1¾ oz/110 yds/50g per ball):
  1 ball #201 rainbow
- Lion Brand Fun Fur bulky (chunky) weight yarn (1¾ oz/60 yds/50g per ball):
  1 ball #194 lime
- Lion Brand Microspun light (DK) weight yarn (2½ oz/168 yds/70g per ball):
  1 ball #194 lime
- Sizes G/6/4mm and P/15mm crochet hooks or size needed to obtain gauge
- Tapestry needle
- 1-inch pin back

Gauge
Size P hook: Rnds 1 & 2 = 3½ inches

Special Stitch
Picot: Ch 3, sl st in 3rd ch from hook.

Flower
Rnd 1: With size P hook and rainbow, ch 4, 13 sc in 4th ch from hook, join with sl st in beg sc. *(13 sc)*

Rnd 2: Picot *(see Special Stitch)*, [sl st in next st, picot] around, join with sl st in joining sl st on last rnd. Fasten off.

Center
With size G hook, holding 1 strand of Fun Fur and 1 strand of Microspun tog, ch 4, 5 dc in 4th ch from hook, drop lp from hook, insert hook in top of 4th ch of beg ch-4, pull dropped lp through, ch 1. Fasten off.
Sew to center of Flower.
Sew pin back to back of Flower.

KATHY

EASY

Finished Size

3½ inches in diameter

Materials

MEDIUM

- Bernat Satin medium (worsted) weight yarn (3½ oz/163 yds/100g per skein):
  ¼ oz/12 yds/7g each #04317 star dust, #04732 mai tai and #04236 evergreen
- Size G/6/4mm crochet hook or size needed to obtain gauge
- Tapestry needle
- Sewing needle
- Sewing thread
- Raspberry glass beads: 5
- 1-inch pin back

Gauge

Rnds 1 & 2 = 2 inches

Special Stitches

Beginning cluster (beg cl): Ch 3 *(counts as first dc)*, holding back last lp of each st on hook, 3 dc in same st, yo, pull through all lps on hook, ch 3, sl st in same st.
Cluster (cl): Holding back last lp of each st on hook, 4 dc in next st, yo, pull through all lps on hook.

Flower

Rnd 1: With star dust, ch 2, 9 sc in 2nd ch from hook, join with sl st in **front lp** *(see Stitch Guide)* of beg sc. *(9 sc)*
Rnd 2: Beg cl *(see Special Stitches)* in front lp of first st *(petal)*, (sl st, ch 3, **cl**–*see Special Stitches*, ch 3, sl st) in front lp of each st around, join with sl st in joining sl st of last rnd. Fasten off. *(9 petals)*
Rnd 3: Working in **back lp** *(see Stitch Guide)* of sts on rnd 1, join mai tai with sl st in first sc, ch 9, sl st in same st *(petal)*, [(sl st, ch 9, sl st) in next sc] around, join with sl st in beg sl st. Fasten off. *(9 petals)*
Rnd 4: Join evergreen with sl st between any 2 petals, [ch 5, sl st in 2nd ch from hook, sc in next ch, hdc in next ch, dc in next ch, sl st between same petal and next petal] 8 times, ch 5, sl st in 2nd ch from hook, sc in next ch, hdc in next ch, dc in next ch, join with sl st in beg sl st. Fasten off.

Finishing

Thread beads onto sewing thread. Tie ends of thread tog, pulling beads into circle.
Sew circle of beads to center of Flower.
Sew pin back to back of Flower.

SAHEYO

EASY

Finished Size

5½ inches in diameter

Materials

- Lion Brand Homespun bulky (chunky) weight yarn (6 oz/185 yds/170g per skein): ¼ oz/8 yds/7g #311 rococo
- Size G/6/4mm crochet hook or size needed to obtain gauge
- Tapestry needle
- Sewing needle
- Sewing thread
- 1 large wooden bead
- 9 small wooden beads
- 6-inch piece faux leather fringe

Gauge

Rnd 1 = 1 inch

Flower

Center

Ch 2, 10 sc in 2nd ch from hook, join with sl st in beg sc. *(10 sc)*

First Petal

Row 1: Ch 1, hdc in first st, 2 hdc in next st, leaving rem sts unworked, turn. *(3 hdc)*
Row 2: Ch 1, 2 hdc in each st across, turn. *(6 hdc)*
Row 3: Ch 1, **hdc dec** *(see Stitch Guide)* in first 2 sts, hdc in each of next 2 sts, hdc dec in last 2 sts, turn. *(4 hdc)*
Row 4: Ch 1, [hdc dec in next 2 sts] twice, turn. *(2 hdc)*
Row 5: Ch 1, hdc dec in 2 sts. Fasten off.

Next Petal

Row 1: Join with sl st in next unworked sc on Center, ch 1, hdc in same st, 2 hdc in next st, leaving rem sts unworked, turn. *(3 hdc)*

Rows 2–5: Rep rows 2–5 of First Petal.
Rep Next Petal 3 times for total of 5 Petals.

Beaded Trim

Cut 20-inch length of yarn and tie knot in 1 end. [Thread small bead on yarn, tie knot in yarn at top of bead] 9 times. Trim ends.

Finishing

1. Sew center of Beaded Trim between any 2 petals as shown in photo.
2. Roll leather fringe tightly and insert in center of Flower. Using sewing needle and sewing thread sew to back of Flower.
3. Sew large bead to center of Flower. ■

FOILED HEART NECKLACE

DESIGN BY MARY LAYFIELD

EASY

Finished Size

One size fits most

Materials

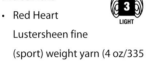

- Red Heart Lustersheen fine (sport) weight yarn (4 oz/335 yds/113g per skein):
    1 skein #2 black
- Size B/1/2.25mm crochet hook or size needed to obtain gauge
- Sewing needle
- Sewing thread
- Accessories from Blue Moon Bead Co.:
    14 clear E-beads with 8mm foil beads
    1 large #65406 red/black foil heart
    1 package #64116 matching red/black foil 8mm beads
    Silver hook and eye

Special Stitch

Cross-stitch (cross-st): Sk next st, dc in next st, dc in st just sk.

NECKLACE

Row 1: Ch 97, sc in 2nd ch from hook and in each ch across, turn.

Row 2: Ch 3 *(counts as first dc)*, dc in next st, **cross-st** *(see Special Stitch)*, [dc in next st, cross-st, dc in next st, cross-st, 2 dc in next st, cross-st] 4 times, [dc in next st, cross-st] 5 times, [2 dc in next st, cross-st, dc in next st, cross-st, dc in next st, cross-st] 4 times, 2 dc in next st, cross-st, dc in each of last 2 sts, **do not turn**. Fasten off. Attach hook and eye to ends of row 1.

Row 3: Sk first 31 sts, join with sc in next st, ch 10, sk next 3 sts, sc in next st, ch 16, sk next 13 sts, sc in next st, (dc, ch 2, dc) in next st *(center)*, ch 16, sk next 13 sts, sc in next st, ch 10, sk next 3 sts, sc in each of next 2 sts leaving rem sts unworked, turn.

Row 4: Sc in each of next 10 chs, sc in each of first 2 chs of ch-16, ch 8, sk next 3 chs, sc in next ch, ch 9, sk next 4 chs, sc in next ch, ch 14, sc in 6th ch of next ch-16, ch 9, sk next 4 chs, sc in next ch, ch 8, sk next 3 chs, sc in each of last 2 chs, sc in each of next 10 chs, sc in next st on row 2. Fasten off.

Row 5: Working across chs of ch-14, join with sc in first ch, sc in each of next 5 chs, ch 9, sk next 2 chs, sc in each of last 6 chs. Fasten off.

Sew beads to Necklace as shown in photo or as desired. ∎

HOT PANTS SET CONTINUED FROM PAGE 91

Neck & Shoulder Shaping

Row 1: Sl st in first sc, sc in each rem sc across, sc in beg ch-1 of previous row, turn.

Row 2: Ch 1, sk first sc, sc in each st across, turn, do not work in ch-1 sp of previous row at neck edge.

Rep rows 1 and 2 alternately until 10 [10, 11, 12, 13] sts rem.

Rows 3–14: Ch 1, sc in each st across, turn. At the end of last rep, fasten off.

Right Front Armhole

Row 1: Attach pink in 33rd st from Right Front edge, ch 1, sc in each of next 17 [17, 22, 27, 27] sts, inc in next st, sc in each rem st across, turn.

For Sizes X-Small, Small & Medium Only

Row 2: Ch 1, sc in each of next 15 [15, 20] sts, 2 sc in next sc, sc in each rem sc across, turn.

Row 3: Ch 1, sc in each of next 18 [18, 23] sts, 2 sc in next st, sc in next st, 2 sc in next st, sc in each rem st across, turn.

For Sizes Large & X-Large Only

Row 2: Ch 1, sc in each of next 28 [28] sts, 2 sc in next st, sc in each rem st across, turn.

Row 3: Ch 1, sc in each st to within 1 st before inc on previous row, 2 sc in next st, sc in next st, 2 sc in next st, sc in each rem sc across to armhole, turn.

For All Sizes

Rows 4–10: Rep rows 4–10 of Left Front Armhole, working inc and dec sts.

Neck & Shoulder Shaping

Row 1: Ch 1, sc across, turn, do not work in ch-1 of previous row at neck edge.

Row 2: Sk first st, sc in each st across, sc in beg ch-1 of previous row, turn.

Rep rows 1 and 2 alternately until 10 [10, 11, 12, 13] sts rem.

Rows 3–14: Ch 1, sc in each st across, turn. At the end of last rep, fasten off.

Back

Row 1: With RS facing, attach pink in the 8th st from beg of armhole edge of Right Front, ch 1, sc in each st across to last 8 sts of Left Front, turn.

Row 2: Ch 1, sc in each st across, turn, do not work in turning ch-1 of previous row.

Rep row 2 until back measures 10 inches from beg.

First Back Neck

Note: Place marker at center Back stitch.

Row 1: Ch 1, sc in same st as beg ch-1, sc in each st to marked st, turn.

Row 2: Ch 1, do not work in same st with beg ch-1 at neck edge, sc in each rem st across, turn.

Row 3: Ch 1, sc in each st across, turn.

Rep rows 2 and 3 alternately until Back measures 10 inches.

Row 4: With size F hook, work block st across row, turn.

Row 5: With size G hook, ch 1, sc in each st across.

Row 6: Holding WS of Front and Back Shoulders tog and working through both thicknesses, sl st in front lps only across, fasten off.

2nd Back Neck

Row 1: Attach pink in next st after marked st at center Back, ch 1, sc in same st as beg ch-1, sc in each st across, turn.

Row 2: Ch 1, sc in each st across, do not work in same st as beg ch-1 at neck edge, turn.

Row 3: Ch 1, sc in each st across, turn.

Rep rows 2 and 3 alternately until Back measures 10 inches.

Row 4: With size F hook, work block st across, turn.

Row 5: With size G hook, ch 1, sc in each st across. Fasten off.

Row 6: Holding WS of Front and Back Shoulders tog and working through both thicknesses, sl st in front lps only across, fasten off.

Armhole Trim

Rnd 1: With size G hook, attach pink at underarm, ch 1, sc evenly spaced around armhole opening, join in beg sc, fasten off.

Rep on opposite armhole.

Neckline Trim

Row 1: With size G hook, attach pink in Right Front neck edge in first row without an inc, sc evenly spaced up neckline across Back Neckline and to opposite side of Left Front, ending in last row of neckline without inc sts, fasten off.

Row 2: With size G hook, attach beige with sl st 1 st before previous row, sc in each sc of previous row, sl st in next st, fasten off.

Bottom Trim

Row 1: With size G hook, attach beige in Left Front bottom edge and working across opposite side of foundation ch, ch 1, sc in each st across bottom edge of Top, fasten off.

Drawstring

With size F hook and beige, make a ch to desired length and lace through ends of every other row beg at lower edge just above block st row, up to first dec row of center front, tie ends in a bow. ■

KIWI VEST & HEADBAND CONTINUED FROM PAGE 92

hook, ch 16, sl st in 2nd ch from hook, sl st in each rem ch across, turn.

Rows 1–12: Rep rows 1–12 of Right Front.

Neck & Armhole Shaping

Row 13: Rep row 13 of Neck and Armhole Shaping. Rep row 13 until Back measures 6½ inches from first inc, ending at armhole edge, turn. *(31 sts)*

Row 14: At armhole edge, ch 13, sl st in 2nd ch from hook, sl st in each ch, sl st loosely in last st made before ch-13, continue in pattern across to last 2 sts, turn.

Row 15: Work even in pattern across, turn. Rep row 15 until Back measures 4 inches from armhole.

Row 16: Rep row 17 of Right Front.

Row 17: Rep row 18 of Right Front. Rep rows 16 and 17 until 3 sts rem.

Row 18: Ch 2, sk 1 st, hdc in next st, fasten off.

Assembly

Holding RS of Backs tog and working through both

thicknesses, sc Backs tog across the 4-inch section worked straight at center back.

Holding RS of Front and Back tog at shoulders, sc through both thicknesses. Holding sides tog, sc through both thicknesses of each side seam.

Outer Trim

Rnd 1: With RS facing and size F [G, H] hook, attach yarn at side seam, ch 1, sc evenly spaced around entire outer edge, working 2 sc in each outer point of Vest, join in beg sc, fasten off.

Tie

With size F [G, H] hook, ch 100, fasten off.
Insert 1 end of ch from from front to back through right front center point, insert same end from back to front through left front center point, pull ends even, tie ends in a bow.

HEADBAND

Row 1: With size G hook, ch 101, sl st loosely in 2nd ch from hook, hdc in next ch, [sl st loosely in next ch, hdc in next ch] across, turn.

Row 2: Ch 1, working in back lps only, [sl st loosely in hdc, hdc in next sl st] across, turn.
Rep row 2 until Headband is 1¾ inches wide. At the end of last rep, do not fasten off.

Trim & Ties

Rnd 1: Ch 1, sc in each st across last row, *ch 35, sl st in 2nd ch from hook, sl st in each rem ch across *(Tie)*, sc in same st as last sc, sc evenly spaced across ends of rows, ch 35, sl st in 2nd ch from hook, sl st in each rem ch across *(Tie)*, sc in same st as last sc, sc evenly spaced across opposite side of foundation ch, rep between *, join in beg sc, fasten off.
When wearing Headband, tie strands tog in a bow at back neckline. ■

LADDER-STITCH CLOCHE CONTINUED FROM PAGE 95

Rnd 17: Sl st into ch-2 sp, ch 1, (sc, ch 2, sc) in same ch-2 sp, ch 1, sk next ch-2 sp, [(sc, ch 2, sc) in next ch-2 sp, ch 1, sk next ch-2 sp] around, join in beg sc, fasten off.

FLOWER

Rnd 1: With eggplant, ch 4, join in first ch to form a ring, ch 1, 8 sc in ring, join in beg sc. *(8 sc)*
Rnd 2: [Ch 3, sl st in next sc] 8 times, fasten off. *(8 ch-3 sps)*
Rnd 3: Draw up a lp of olive in any ch-3 sp, ch 1, (sc, 3 dc, sc) in same ch-3 sp and in each rem ch-3 sp around, join in beg sc, leaving an 8-inch length, fasten off.
Position Flower at joining seam of rnd 14 of Cloche and sew in place using tapestry needle and 8-inch length. ■

EARTH CHILD CONTINUED FROM PAGE 101

Small Ring

Make 3.

Rnd 1: Attach linen to ¾-inch metal ring, ch 1, work 20 sc over ring, join in beg sc, leaving a length for sewing, fasten off. *(20 sc)*

Finishing

Using rem lengths and yarn needle, sew Large Ring to row 33 of Neckband and 1 Small Ring to row 24 and row 42. Sew a Small Ring to the center bottom of the Large Ring.

Cut a 16-inch length of linen, fold length in half and with yarn needle pass the linen length through an 18mm bead. Tie a double knot in ends to keep bead from slipping off. With yarn needle attach loose ends to center bottom of Small Ring, tie at back to secure, fasten off. Attach one 18mm bead to each rem Small Ring. Weave in all loose ends.

BRACELET

Small Ring

Make 4.

Rnd 1: Attach linen to rem ¾-inch metal rings, ch 1, 20 sc over ring, join in first sc, fasten off. *(20 sc)*

Finishing

With yarn needle and a long length of linen, pass through a 28mm bead and sew each loose end of linen passed through bead to Small Ring. Continue to sew beads and Small Rings alternately tog forming a strip, ending with sewing last Small Ring to first bead to form a closed circle. Weave in all loose ends. ∎

GRANNY SQUARE SHRINK VEST CONTINUED FROM PAGE 102

Rnd 4: Ch 6 *(counts as first dc, ch-3)*, sk next dc, [dc in next dc, ch 3, sk next dc] around, join in 3rd ch of beg ch-6. *(16 dc, 16 ch-3 sps)*

Rnd 5: Ch 3, 4 dc in next ch-3 sp, [dc in next dc, 4 dc in next ch-3 sp] around, join in 3rd ch of beg ch-3. *(80 dc)*

For Size X-Small Only

Rnd 6: Ch 1, sc in joining, sc in next dc, *ch 3, sk next 2 dc, hdc in next dc, ch 3, sk next 2 dc, dc in next dc, ch 3, sk next 2 dc, (dc, ch 2, tr, ch 2, dc) in next dc, ch 3, sk next 2 dc, dc in next dc, ch 3, sk next 2 dc, hdc in next dc, ch 3, sk next 2 dc, sc in each of next 3 dc, rep from * around, ending with sc in last dc, join in beg sc.

Rnd 7: Ch 3, sk first sc, dc in next sc, *2 dc in next ch-3 sp, dc in next hdc, [2 dc in next ch-3 sp, dc in next dc] twice, 2 dc in next ch-3 sp, tr in next tr, [2 dc in next ch-3 sp, dc in next dc] twice, 2 dc in next ch-3 sp, dc in next hdc, 2 dc in next ch-3 sp, dc in each of next 3 sc, rep from * around, ending with dc in last sc, join in top of beg ch-3, fasten off.

For Sizes Small, Medium, Large & X-Large Only
Rnd 6: Ch 3, dc in each dc around, join in 3rd ch of beg ch-3.

Rnd 7: Ch 1, sc in joining, sc in next dc, *ch 3, sk next 2 dc, hdc in next dc, ch 3, sk next 2 dc, dc in next dc, ch 4, sk next 2 dc, tr in next dc, ch 4, sk next 2 dc, dc in next dc, ch 3, sk next 2 dc, hdc in next dc, ch 3, sk next 2 dc, sc in each of next 3 dc, rep from * around, ending with sk next 2 dc, sc in last dc, join in beg sc.

Rnd 8: Ch 1, sc in joining, sc in next sc, *2 sc in next ch-3 sp, sc in next hdc, ch 3, dc in next dc, ch 3, (tr, {ch 2, tr} twice) in next tr, ch 3, dc in next dc, ch 3, sc in next hdc, 2 sc in next ch-3 sp**, sc in each of next 3 sc, rep from *

around, ending last rep at **, sc in last sc, join in beg sc.

Rnd 9: Ch 3, dc in each of next 4 sc, *3 dc in next ch-3 sp, dc in next dc, 4 dc in next ch-3 sp, dc in next tr, 3 dc in next ch-2 sp, tr in next tr, 3 dc in next ch-2 sp, dc in next tr, 4 dc in next ch-3 sp, dc in next dc, 3 dc in next ch-3 sp, dc in each of next 9 sc, rep from * around, ending with dc in each of next 4 sc, join in 3rd ch of beg ch-3, fasten off sizes small and medium only. *(136 dc)*

For Size Large Only
Rnd 10: Ch 3, dc in each dc around, working (dc, tr, dc) in each corner tr, join in 3rd ch of beg ch-3, fasten off.

For Size X-Large Only
Rnds 10 & 11: Ch 3, dc in each dc around, working (dc, tr, dc) in each corner tr, join in 3rd ch of beg ch-3, fasten off.

First Front Side Panel
For All Sizes
Row 1: With RS facing, attach yarn on bottom right in corner tr, ch 1, sc in same st as joining, sc in each of next 20 [25, 28, 31, 34] sts, turn. *(21 [26, 29, 32, 35] sc)*

Row 2: Ch 1, sc in first sc, **sc dec** *(see Stitch Guide)* in next 2 sts, sc in each rem st across, turn. *(20 [25, 28, 31, 34] sc)*

Row 3: Ch 1, sc in each st across to last 3 sts, sc dec in next 2 sts, sc in last st, turn. *(19 [24, 27, 30, 34] sc)*

For Size X-Small Only
Row 4: Rep row 2, fasten off. *(18 sc)*

For Size Small Only
Rows 4 & 5: Rep rows 2 and 3. *([22] sc)*
Row 6: Rep row 2, fasten off. *([21] sc)*

For Size Medium Only
Rows 4–7: [Rep rows 2 and 3 alternately] twice. At the end of last rep, fasten off. *([23] sc)*

For Size Large Only
Rows 4–7: [Rep rows 2 and 3 alternately] twice. *([26] sc)*
Rows 8–10: Ch 1, sc in each st across, turn. At the end of last rep, fasten off.

For Size X-Large Only

Rows 4–9: [Rep rows 2 and 3 alternately] 3 times. *([28] sc)*

Rows 10–14: Ch 1, sc in each st across, turn. At the end of last rep, fasten off.

2nd Front Side Panel

Rows 1–4 [1–6, 1–7, 1–10, 1–14]: Rep rows 1–4 [1–6, 1–7, 1–10, 1–14] of First Front Side Panel.

First & 2nd Back Side Panels

Rep First and 2nd Front Side Panels.

Strap

Make 2 each front & back.

Row 1: With RS facing, join yarn at upper right tr, ch 1, sc in same st as joining and in each of next 4 [5, 5, 6, 6] sts, turn. *(5 [6, 6, 7, 7] sc)*

Row 2: Ch 1, sc in each sc across, turn.

Rows 3–9 [3–9, 3–10, 3–12, 3–14]: Rep Row 2. At the end of last rep, fasten off.

With RS facing, join yarn in 5th [6th, 6th, 7th, 7th] st from left corner tr, rep rows 1–9 [1–9, 1–10, 1–12, 1–14].

With RS tog, matching sts and sewing through top lps only, sew shoulders tog. With RS tog, sew side seams.

Bottom Edging

Rnd 1 (WS): Attach yarn at side seam, ch 1, sc evenly spaced around, join in beg sc, turn.

Rnds 2–4: Ch 1, sc in each sc around, join in beg sc. At the end of last rep, fasten off.

Armhole Trim

Rnd 1 (RS): Attach yarn at underarm, ch 1, sc evenly spaced around, working sc dec where the strap joins each Front and Back to keep piece flat, join in beg sc, fasten off.

Rep on opposite armhole opening.

Neckline Trim

Rnd 1 (RS): Attach yarn at shoulder seam, ch 1, sc evenly spaced around, working sc dec at 4 corners where the strap joins each Front and Back to keep piece flat, join in beg sc, fasten off. ■

LACY PINEAPPLES SHELL CONTINUED FROM PAGE 123

Row 3: Ch 4, tr in each ch-1 sp and each hdc across, turn.

Rows 4–19: [Rep rows 2 and 3 alternately] 8 times.

Row 20: Sl st in each of next 6 sts, ch 3, sk next st, hdc in next st, [ch 1, sk next st, hdc in next st] 42 times, leaving last 6 sts unworked, turn. *(43 hdc)*

Row 21: Rep row 3. *(85 tr)*

First Strap

Row 1: Ch 3, sk next st, hdc in next st, [ch 1, sk next st, hdc in next st] 6 times, turn. *(8 hdc)*

Row 2: Ch 4, tr in each ch-1 sp and each hdc across, turn.

Rows 3–10: [Rep rows 1 and 2 alternately] 4 times. At the end of last rep, fasten off.

2nd Strap

Row 1: Sk next 55 sts of row 21 of back panel, join with sl st in next st, ch 3, sk next st, hdc in next st, [ch 1, sk next st, hdc in next st] 6 times, turn. *(8 hdc)*

Row 2: Rep row 2 of First Strap.

Rows 3–10: [Rep rows 1 and 2 of First Strap alternately] 4 times.

Front Panel

Row 1: With size C [D, E, F] hook, ch 100, tr in 5th ch from hook, tr in each of next 13 chs, dc in each of next 15 chs, hdc in each of next 16 chs, sc in each of next 5 chs, hdc in each of next 16 chs, dc in each of next 15 chs, tr in each of next 15 chs, turn. *(5 sc, 32 hdc, 30 dc, 30 tr)*

Row 2: Ch 3, sk next st, [hdc in next st, ch 1, sk next st] 22 times, hdc in each of next 5 sts, [ch 1, sk next st, hdc in next st] across, turn. *(51 hdc)*

Row 3: Ch 4, [tr in next ch-1 sp, tr in next st] 7 times, dc in next ch-1 sp, [dc in next st, dc in next ch-1 sp] 7 times, [hdc in next st, hdc in next ch-1 sp] 8 times, sc in each of next 5 sts, [hdc in next ch-11 sp, hdc in next st] 8 times, dc in next ch-1 sp, [dc in next st, dc in next ch-1 sp] 7 times, tr in next st, [tr in next ch-1 sp, tr in next st] across, turn.

Row 4: Rep row 2.

Row 5: Ch 4, tr in each of next 45 sts, sc in each of next 5 sts, tr in each rem st across, turn. *(5 sc, 92 tr)*

Row 6: Rep row 2.

Rows 7–18: [Rep rows 3–6 consecutively] 3 times.

Row 19: Rep row 3.

Row 20: Sl st in each of next 6 sts, ch 3, sk next st, [hdc in next st, ch 1, sk next st] 19 times, ch 1, sk next st, hdc in each of next 5 sts, [ch 1, sk next st, hdc in next st] across to last 6 sts, leaving rem 6 sts unworked, turn. *(45 hdc)*

Row 21: Rep row 5.

Row 22: Ch 3, sk next st, [hdc in next st, ch 1, sk next st] 19 times, hdc in each of next 5 sts, [ch 1, sk next st, hdc in next st] across, turn. *(45 hdc)*

Row 23: Ch 4, [tr in next ch-1 sp, tr in next st] 6 times, [dc in next ch-1 sp, dc in next st] 6 times, [hdc in next ch-1 sp, hdc in next st] 4 times, [sk next ch-1 sp, hdc in next st] 3 times, hdc in next ch-1 sp, sc in each of next 5 sts, hdc in next ch-1 sp, [hdc in next st, sk next ch-1 sp] 3 times, [hdc in next st, hdc in next ch-1 sp] 4 times, [dc in next st, dc in next ch-1 sp] 6 times, [tr in next st, tr in next ch-1 sp] 6 times, tr in last st, turn. *(5 sc, 24 hdc, 24 dc, 25 tr)*

Row 24: Ch 3, sk next st, [hdc in next st, ch 1, sk next

st] 17 times, hdc in each of next 5 sts, [ch 1, sk next st, hdc in next st] across, turn. *(43 hdc)*

Row 25: Ch 4, tr in next ch-1 sp, [tr in next st, tr in next ch-1 sp] 17 times, sc in each of next 5 sts, [tr in next ch-1 sp, tr in next st] across, turn. *(5 sc, 74 tr)*

Row 26: Rep row 24.

Row 27: Ch 4, [tr in next ch-1 sp, tr in next tr] 6 times, [dc in next ch-1 sp, dc in next st] 6 times, [hdc in next ch-1 sp, hdc in next st] 6 times, sc in each of next 5 sts, [hdc in next ch-1 sp, hdc in next st] 6 times, [dc in next st, dc in next ch-1 sp] 6 times, tr in next st, [tr in next ch-1 sp, tr in next st] 6 times, turn. *(5 sc, 24 hdc, 24 dc, 26 tr)*

Row 28: Rep row 24.

Row 29: Rep row 25.

Row 30: Ch 3, [sk next st, hdc in next st] 10 times, [**sc dec** *(see Stitch Guide)* in next 2 sts] 8 times, sc in each of next 5 sts, [sc dec in next 2 sts] 8 times, [sk next st, hdc in next st] across, fasten off. *(21 sc, 22 hdc)*

First Strap

Row 1: Working around post of last sts of rows 25–30, join with sl st in row 25, ch 2, 2 hdc in same sp, 2 hdc in next row, [3 hdc in next row, 2 hdc in next row] twice, turn. *(15 hdc)*

Row 2: Ch 3, sk next st, hdc in next st, [ch 1, sk next st, hdc in next st] across, turn. *(8 hdc)*

Row 3: Ch 4, [tr in next ch-1 sp, tr in next st] across, turn. *(15 tr)*

Rows 4–9: [Rep rows 2 and 3 alternately] 3 times.

Row 10: Rep row 2, leaving a long length for sewing, fasten off.

Sew last row of this strap to last row of strap on Back.

2nd Strap

Row 1: Working around post of last sts of rows 25–30, join with sl st in row 30, ch 2, hdc in same sp, 2 hdc in next row, [3 hdc in next row, 2 hdc in next row] twice, turn. *(15 hdc)*

Rows 2–10: Rep rows 2–10 of First Strap.

Assembly

Matching row ends, stitch side seams attaching Front and Back Panels. With RS tog, center Front Panel with

Strips 1 and 2 in the middle of Front Panel, st seam tog attaching Front and Back Panels to Strips.

Armhole Trim

Rnd 1: With size C [D, E, F] hook, join with sc in first unworked st at underarm, sc in each of next 11 sts, working in row ends around opening, work 2 sc into each row end, join in beg sc. *(66 sc)*

Rnd 2: Ch 1, sc in same st, sk next 2 sts, 6 dc in next st, sk next 2 sts, [sc in next st, sk next 2 sts, 6 dc in next st, sk next 2 sts] around, join in beg sc, fasten off. Rep on opposite armhole.

Neckline Trim

Rnd 1: Join with sc in first ch-1 sp on row 30 of Front Panel, sc in each of next 9 ch-1 sps, sc in each of next 21 sts, sc in each of next 10 ch-1 sps, working in row ends of Strap, work 2 sc into each row and 1 sc into seam, working in sts across back, [sc in each of next 4 sts, sc dec in next 2 sts] 4 times, [sc in next st, sc dec in next 2 sts] 3 times, [sc in each of next 4 sts, sc dec in next 2 sts] 3 times, sc in each of next 4 sts, working in row ends of 2nd Strap, work 2 sc into each row and 1 sc into seam, join in beg sc. *(168 sc)*

Rnd 2: Ch 3, 5 dc in same st, [sk next 2 sts, sc in next st, sk next 2 sts, 6 dc in next st] 5 times, [sk next 2 sts, sc in next st] twice, sk next st, sl st in next st, sk next st, sc in next st, [sk next 2 sts, 6 dc in next st, sk next 2 sts, sc in next st, sk next 2 sts] around, join in beg sc, fasten off. ■

SHORT & SEXY TANK CONTINUED FROM PAGE 131

For Sizes Large & X-Large Only

Row 58 [62]: Ch 1, sc dec in next 2 sc, sc in each of next 14 [19] sts, sc in back lps only of next 18 [18] sts, turn. *([33, 38] sts)*

Row 59 [63]: Ch 1, working in back lps only, sc in each of next 18 [18] sts, sc in each of next 15 [20] sts, turn. *([33, 38] sts)*

For Size Large Only

Rows 60–116: Rep rows 2–58. At the end of last rep, turn.

For Size X-Large Only

Row 64: Ch 1, sc dec in next 2 sc, sc in each of next 17 sts, working in back lps only, sc in each of next 18 sts, turn. *([36] sts)*

Row 65: Ch 1, working in back lps, sc in each of next 18 sts only, sc in each of next 18 sts, turn. *([36] sts)*

Rows 66–128: Rep rows 2–64. At the end of last rep, turn.

Joining

Loosely sl st last row of Tank to first row. Fasten off. Sl st shoulder seams closed. Fasten off after each shoulder.

Armhole Border

Rnd 1 (RS): Attach 2 strands at underarm, ch 1, sc evenly spaced around opening, join in beg sc, fasten off. Rep on opposite armhole.

Neckline Border

Rnd 1 (RS): Attach 2 strands at shoulder seam, ch 1, sc evenly spaced around opening, working sc dec at corners to keep edges flat, join in beg sc, fasten off. ∎

WRAP-TIE TOP CONTINUED FROM PAGE 140

2nd Shoulder Shaping

Row 39 [43, 47, 51]: Sk next 15 sts of row 38 [42, 46, 50], attach yarn in next st, ch 2, work in Pattern Stitch across rem sts, turn. *(10 [12, 14, 16] sts)*

Row 40 [44, 48, 52]: Ch 2, work in Pattern Stitch across 10 [12, 14, 16] sts, fasten off.

Right Front

Row 25 [29, 33, 37]: Attach yarn in next unworked st of row 24 [28, 32, 36], ch 2, dc in same st as beg ch-2, Pattern Stitch across row to last 3 sts, sc in next st, hdc dec in next 2 sts, turn. *(15 [17, 19, 21] sts)*

Row 26 [30, 34, 38]: Work row 2 of Pattern Stitch.

Row 27 [31, 35, 39]: Work row 2 of Pattern Stitch across to last 2 sts, hdc dec in last 2 sts, turn. *(14 [16, 18, 20] sts)*

Row 28 [32, 36, 40]: Rep row 2 of Pattern Stitch.

Row 29 [33, 37, 41]: Rep row 27 [31, 35, 39]. *(13 [15, 17, 19] sts)*

Rows 30–35 [34–39, 38–43, 42–47]: [Rep rows 28 and 29 {32 and 33, 36 and 37, 40 and 41} alternately] 3 times. *(10 [12, 14, 16] sts)*

Rows 36–40 [40–44, 44–48, 48–52]: Rep row 2 of Pattern Stitch. At the end of last rep, fasten off.

Sleeve

Rnd 1: With RS facing, attach yarn at underarm, ch 2, work 34 [34, 36, 36] sc evenly spaced around, join in beg sc, turn. *(34 [34, 36, 36] sc)*

Rnd 2: Ch 1, [sc in next st, dc in next st] around, join in beg sc, turn.

Rnd 3: Ch 1, [sc in each dc, dc in each sc] around, join in beg sc, turn.

Rnds 4–7: Rep rnd 3. At the end of rnd 7, do not turn.

Rnd 8: Ch 1, sc in each sc and each dc around, join in beg sc, fasten off.

Rep on opposite underarm.

Border & Ties

Rnd 1: With RS facing, attach yarn on bottom edge in any st of Back, keeping st markers on each front edge,

ch 1, sc evenly spaced around outer edge, working 5 sc in center of each bottom corner, join in beg sc, do not turn.

Rnd 2: Ch 1, sc in each sc around, working 5 sc in center sc of each 5-sc group and working **sc dec** *(see Stitch Guide)* in each marked st on each side of Front, join in beg sc, do not turn.

Rnd 3: Ch 1, sc in each sc to first 5-sc corner, sc in each of next 2 sc, sl st in next sc, ch 81 *(approximately 30 inches long)*, sc in 2nd ch from hook, sc in each rem ch across, sl st in same sc as first sl st *(first Tie)*, sc in each

rem st to st marker, working sc dec at each st marker to next 5-sc corner, sc in each of next 2 sc, sl st in next sc, ch 81, sc in 2nd ch from hook, sc in each rem ch across, sl st in same sc as first sl st *(2nd Tie)*, sc in each rem sc around, join in beg sc, do not turn.

Rnd 4: Ch 1, sc in each sc around to first Tie, *work 2 sc in st before the Tie, holding Tie to front and working behind Tie, work 2 sc in next sc after Tie*, sc in each sc to next Tie, rep between *, sc in each rem st around, join in beg sc, fasten off. ■

CANYON COLORS HAT & SCARF CONTINUED FROM PAGE 152

Rnds 7–9: Rep rnd 3. *(46 dc)*

Rnd 10: Fold elastic thread in 4 strands and tie tog at each end, while leaving an end, hold the 4 strands tog and working over elastic strands, rep rnd 3, fasten off. Weave rem ends of elastic into Hat.

Fur Trim

Rnd 1: With WS facing, attach 2 strands of champagne in any dc of rnd 10, ch 1, sc in same dc as beg ch-1, sc in each dc around, do not join, place marker to mark rnds as work progresses. *(46 sc)*

Rnd 2: Sc in each sc around.

Rnds 3–7: Rep rnd 2. At the end of rnd 7, sl st in next st, fasten off. ■

General Instructions

Please review the following information before working the projects in this book. Important details about the abbreviations and symbols used are included.

Hooks

Crochet hooks are sized for different weights of yarn and thread. For thread crochet, you will usually use a steel crochet hook. Steel crochet-hook sizes range from size 00 to 14. The higher the number of the hook, the smaller your stitches will be. For example, a size 1 steel crochet hook will give you much larger stitches than a size 9 steel crochet hook. Keep in mind that the sizes given with the pattern instructions were obtained by working with the size thread or yarn and hook given in the materials list. If you work with a smaller hook, depending on your gauge, your finished project size will be smaller; if you work with a larger hook, your finished project size will be larger.

Gauge

Gauge is determined by the tightness or looseness of your stitches, and affects the finished size of your project. If you are concerned about the finished size of the project matching the size given, take time to crochet a small section of the pattern and then check your gauge. For example, if the gauge called for is 10 dc = 1 inch, and your gauge is 12 dc to the inch, you should switch to a larger hook. On the other hand, if your gauge is only 8 dc to the inch, you should switch to a smaller hook.

If the gauge given in the pattern is for an entire motif, work one motif and then check your gauge.

Understanding Symbols

As you work through a pattern, you'll quickly notice several symbols in the instructions. These symbols are used to clarify the pattern for you: brackets [], curlicue braces {}, parentheses () and asterisks *.

Brackets [] are used to set off a group of instructions worked a specific number of times. For example, "[ch 3, sc in next ch-3 sp] 7 times" means to work the instructions inside the [] seven times.

Occasionally, a set of instructions inside a set of brackets needs to be repeated, too. In this case, the text within the brackets to be repeated will be set off with curlicue braces {}. For example, "[dc in each of next 3 sts, ch 1, {shell in next ch-1 sp} 3 times, ch 1] 4 times." In this case, in each of the four times you work the instructions included in the brackets, you will work the section included in the curlicue braces three times.

Parentheses () are used to set off a group of stitches to be worked all in one stitch, space or loop. For example, the parentheses () in this set of instructions, "Sk 3 sc, (3 dc, ch 1, 3 dc) in next st" indicate that after skipping 3 sc, you will work 3 dc, ch 1 and 3 more dc all in the next stitch.

Single asterisks * are also used when a group of instructions is repeated. For example, "*Sc in each of the next 5 sc, 2 sc in next sc, rep from * around, join with a sl st in beg sc" simply means you will work the instructions from the first * around the entire round.

Double asterisks ** are used to indicate when a partial set of repeat instructions are to be worked. For example, "*Ch 3, (sc, ch 3, sc) in next ch-2 sp, ch 3**, shell in next dc, rep from * 3 times, ending last rep at **" means that on the third repeat of the single asterisk instructions, you stop at the double asterisks.